TURNING

TURNING

*Reflections on
the Experience of Conversion*

EMILIE GRIFFIN

*Doubleday & Company, Inc.
Garden City, New York
1980*

The author wishes to thank the following publishers for permission to quote from the following works:

C. S. Lewis, THE FOUR LOVES, reprinted with the permission of Harcourt Brace Jovanovich, Inc.

"The Apologist's Evening-Prayer," from POEMS, by C. S. Lewis, © 1964 by the Executors of the Estate of C. S. Lewis. Reprinted by permission of Harcourt Brace Jovanovich, Inc.

SURPRISED BY JOY, © 1955, by C. S. Lewis. Reprinted by permission of Harcourt Brace Jovanovich, Inc.

THE SEVEN STOREY MOUNTAIN, by Thomas Merton, copyright 1948 by Harcourt Brace Jovanovich, Inc.; renewed 1976 by The Trustees of the Merton Legacy Trust. Reprinted by permission of the publishers.

THE GOLDEN STRING, by Bede Griffiths, O.S.B., reprinted with the permission of Macmillan Publishing Co., Inc.

ISBN: 0-385-15823-8
Library of Congress Catalog Card Number 79-6652

081986

For William, who believed;
and for Helen, who understood
everything after all.

ACKNOWLEDGMENTS

It is impossible to thank everyone who has helped me with the writing of this book. However, I would like to make special mention of Rev. John B. Breslin, S.J., my editor at Doubleday; those who were so helpful in reading the manuscript in draft, Rev. Charles Owen Moore, Rev. Michael J. Dempsey, Rev. Burton Everist, Eugene McGovern, Lois Westerlund, and Rev. John R. Willis, S.J.; I owe a special thank-you to Dr. Doris Donnelly for her encouragement; to Rev. William R. Walsh, S.J., whose help has been invaluable; to my husband and my mother, to whom the book is dedicated; and to my children, Lucy, Henry, and Sarah. Each of them made an act of faith in me and so helped me to do what I once thought quite impossible.

FOREWORD

From time to time since I became a Christian, people I have met at random, hearing me speak of the experience, have asked why I did not write something about it. For a long time I had not the slightest intention of doing so. For one thing, I did not want to be argumentative; the apologetics of Sheen and Knox and Chesterton and even of Lewis were not for me. Though my experience had been a high drama to me, I thought it hardly compared with the great stories of conversion already written. Recently, in fact, I heard someone complain that *Surprised by Joy* is not nearly as interesting as, say, the conversion of Augustine or Newman; after all, nothing much "happens" in it. Lewis becomes a Christian, that is all.

But as time went on, I became aware that the experience of conversion—even in a most ordinary life—is worth sharing. Also, as I read more and more stories of conversion—the most recent ones, the ones to be found in magazines like *Guideposts* and on the rack in every airport in America, like Charles Colson's *Born Again*—it seemed to me that in some sense every conversion story is the same story.

It is in fact the story of Abraham, of Moses, of Jacob; the story of Paul. We know the plot in advance; the details differ only in their externals. Nonetheless, since in each case there is a human life at stake, they are worth reading over and over again.

I think, too, I had some hesitation in telling my story because I was afraid that my own failings, the things in my life I have not conquered, even with God's help, would cast a shadow on the truths I love so much. I now think that was not only bad theology, it was also a very definite kind of pride.

So I have come to write this book, which is mostly about converts who have lived in my own lifetime and who have had a powerful influence on me. It is also about myself; but mostly it is intended to be about conversion itself, not in any theoretical way, but in a very practical way (as an experience to be lived and tasted, rather than theorized about).

In a sense, conversion is caught. Sometimes it reaches epidemic proportions as in Colonial America's "Great Awakening," and whole towns and cities and armies "go over" to some set of beliefs or another. Sometimes it goes haywire, as at Jonestown, but that is a matter for psychopathologists, I think.

Lewis called his book *Mere Christianity*, when he wanted to write about the thing itself, plain and simple and without frills. I hope this book, then, will be about mere conversion.

CONTENTS

1
Turning
15

2
Desire
31

3
Dialectic
51

4
Struggle
89

5
Surrender
129

6
Afterwards
151

Bibliography
181

Index
187

TURNING

1
Turning

When I first began to experience the power of God in my own life, I could hardly believe it. Something very real and discernible was happening to me, yet I felt it could not or should not be happening. God was speaking to me; God was calling me. He spoke no louder than a whisper, but I heard him. And each time that I heard him, and chose him, a change occurred, the opening of a door I had not guessed was there. Each step, each crossing of a doorway was made with great uncertainty, my doubts mingling with my faith. But with each step, my strength and my conviction grew; I felt myself on sounder ground. Something was happening in my life, which I could recognize but which I could not yet name. It was conversion.

By conversion I mean the discovery, made gradually or suddenly, that God is real. It is the perception that this real God loves us personally and acts mercifully and justly towards each of us. Conversion is the direct experience of the saving power of God. As such it is not an event, not an action, not an occurrence. Instead it is a continuing revelation and a transforming force. This encounter with the Lord is not one of visions, necessarily, though some converts have experienced God in a mystical way. It is not a matter of sudden changes in the mode of one's life, though some converts do choose new life-styles. Conversion is simply a matter of becoming open to God's overflowing and powerful love. To be filled with that love is to change, to be changed, to act lovingly towards others.

For me, conversion—this turning over of one's life and energies to God—came about first through a slow and hesitant pilgrimage, both intuitive and intellectual. In my journey I was helped by reading first-person accounts by other converts, especially those who were contemporaries or near contemporaries of mine. In their experience I could see my own. The witness given by their stories, and by their willingness to write down their experiences and to publish them, was as persuasive to me as the lives of early Christian martyrs. The resemblance between their struggles and my own gave me the courage to trust my own experience more. I found it helpful, too, to see that these people were dealing, as I was, with the issues of the so-called scientific age; and they were people of learning, intellectuals. They had not thrown reason over in favor of God. Their commitments had been formed out of thought as well as feeling.

The converts who influenced me most at that time were C. S. Lewis, Bede Griffiths, and Thomas Merton. With them I shared a cultural heritage, for all three were English or Irish by nationality or background. They were people of literary bent and intellectuals. This is not to say that these converts were the only influence. I was certainly drawn to the Lord by the example of the practicing Christians I knew. Members of my own family gave me good example by their devotion to the Lord, even though their way was not to be my way. Also, I was driven towards God by convinced agnostics and atheists who failed to persuade me of God's nonexistence. There were other dazzling Christians who influenced me by their writings—Dorothy L. Sayers, G. K. Chesterton, Gerard Manley Hopkins, John Henry Newman—but who were not for me the immediate occasions of grace. And I want to include in particular two other converts who told their own stories in books: Avery Dulles and Dorothy Day. I came upon their stories later on; but each one seemed to parallel my own experience and those of Lewis and Merton and Griffiths.

Before going any further, I think I must explain that it was the inner lives of these people with which I identified so strongly, for their outer lives were very different from my own. Lewis was an Oxford don, whose name was known to me only as the author of a book on my college reading list called *The Allegory of Love*, a book which I had somehow managed not to read. Griffiths, who was Lewis's pupil, was a student of English literature whose conversion carried him into the Roman Catholic Church and then into the monastic life as a Benedictine; Thomas Merton, a student and later a teacher of English, had become first a Roman Catholic and then a Trappist monk; Dulles, a student at Harvard, had entered the Jesuit order; and Day had been a journalist and a social activist both before and after conversion. Externally, their conversion experiences and life situations were very different from mine (apart from the common thread of interest in literature); but when I came to read each of their stories (not knowing, before I read them, anything about their own life paths), I found in them instantaneous friends: people whose cast of mind and whose perception of reality seemed very like my own.

Also it was clear to me from the beginning that their stories were not stories of "how I became a practicing churchman" or "how I became a Roman Catholic" but stories of a personal encounter with God. This was just what was beginning to happen to me. In the ways their paths led them, I saw many parallels to my own experience.

These life stories illustrate one way conversion comes about. Probably the best insight that came to me from reading them was that it was possible to be a believer and an intellectual at the same time. My impression up to that moment was that one must choose between two modes: the rational (leading to atheism or agnosticism) and the religious (leading to a cheerful, unquestioning faith). In this I suppose I was partly a victim of my education. While that education was a good one, it reflected the general attitude of the twentieth-century intellectual community: a tendency to relegate Christianity to the history department.

In my formal education, my exposure to religion had been mediated through literature. I had encountered faith experience in Milton and in Thomas Browne; in Donne and Crashaw and George Herbert and Andrew Marvell; in Emily Dickinson. But (victim of what Lewis calls "chronological snobbery") I had thought of their religion as merely an aspect of their times. I thought it was not their faith which attracted me but imagination itself. I was attracted as much by Donne's secular verse as by his religious poetry; as much by Milton's views on freedom as by his religious themes. I felt also that my attraction to writers of earlier periods might be a defect in myself, a flight from the reality of my own times. I had yet, I thought, to come to grips with my own generation, but in general I did not identify with the experience of twentieth-century writers. I think it worth mentioning that the Bible—one of the great books with which I did identify—was not part of the curriculum in my formal education. In my high school English classes, we had done a bit on Ecclesiastes and something on the Psalms. In college, the King James translation was offered (in brackets) on alternate years, provided that enough students signed up for it. In my education, I think the Bible got less attention as literature than either the *Odyssey* or *Beowulf*. In those days the study of it was thought to be a matter of private faith rather than of general intellectual interest.

So in reading the converts I have mentioned, I came for the first time to twentieth-century intellectuals who took Christianity seriously. In Lewis I found the same appetite which I had for authors of other centuries; but over and above that mere appetite for the past, I also found a willingness to identify with the thought of the ancients and to give it equal weight with the opinions of later thinkers. And this, I think, I had not encountered before. It was as though one could put Plato and Aristotle in a room with Anselm and Aquinas and Camus and Sartre and go about discussing the great issues openly. And this attitude of mind I found attractive; it appealed to my notions of intellectual freedom.

I think the other thing in "my" converts with which I strongly identified was the vigor of their imagination. Each of them had a style of thought which was fundamentally metaphorical: they saw resemblances in things. In fact, each one had used a metaphor as the title for his own spiritual autobiography, and these metaphors seemed, in each instance, to reflect the reality of each conversion.

C. S. Lewis, for example, called his autobiography *Surprised by Joy: The Shape of My Early Life.* This expressed his concept of conversion as an unexpected bounty, something given where nothing was anticipated. Merton, to describe his conversion, borrowed a figure from Dante, the Christian writer who first influenced him, and called his book *The Seven Storey Mountain.* This choice of a figure reflected Merton's insight that conversion is a cleansing and purifying experience, an ascent.

Dorothy Day's title *The Long Loneliness* is not a metaphor, exactly. But this figure—which she takes from the writings of a sixteenth-century English nun—conveys so well the yearning, the longing, which Lewis and others described in their stories as part of what was drawing them towards God.

Bede Griffiths chose his conversion metaphor from a poem of William Blake:

> I will give you the end of a golden string
> Only wind it into a ball
> It will lead you in at heaven's gate
> Built in Jerusalem's wall.[1]

Griffiths called his conversion story *The Golden String.* Throughout the book, Griffiths shows how God's power breaks through the ordinary dimension of our lives, and how this infusion of grace puts into our hands the first clue, the first lead, towards a heavenly destination. A less well-known book by C. S. Lewis, an allegorical work called *The Pilgrim's Regress,* is more than a play on Bunyan's title. It uses as its central metaphor of conversion a turning back, a turning home—in Wordsworth's phrase—"to God, who is our home." Of the conversion books I have mentioned, I think the one by Dulles relies most on the argumentative and reasoning process, yet he too speaks of the intuitive and experiential element within his personal life which led him towards conversion. His central figure is of witness—"it really happened to me"—and he calls his book *A Testimonial to Grace*. In the book, Dulles shows how the use of reason led him to God; but he also tells how much of what happened to him seemed providential, how a seemingly chance event influenced him, how an insight broke through in an otherwise unremarkable afternoon of reading, how the personal encounter with another believer became decisive for him.

When I first began to read such stories I began to see how Christians are models to one another: how the fire of God's love seems to jump from one person to another through the illumination provided by a Christian life. Before that, I had had only a dim understanding of the power of a Christian example. I saw, too, how even the mere reading of the life of a convert might influence another's conversion. I discovered, for instance, how Thomas Merton, surrounded by the power of God operating in the lives of others, made the decision to become a professing Christian and a formal Catholic while reading the letters of Gerard Manley Hopkins, in particular a letter which Hopkins sent to John Henry Newman (not yet Cardinal Newman) stating that he wished to become a Roman Catholic. This event took place in September 1938, when Merton sat reading alone in his room. He describes it this way:

> All of a sudden something began to stir within me, something began to push me, to prompt me. It was a movement that spoke like a voice.

The voice, according to Merton, was not only there, it was very insistent.

> "What are you waiting for?" it said. "Why are you sitting here? Why do you still hesitate? You know what you ought to do. Why don't you do it?"

However much Merton tried to crush this apparent irrationality, the inner prompting would not go away. When he returned to his book, he found the prompting stronger than ever. Finally he got into his coat and walked nine blocks to Corpus Christi Church. As he walked he experienced a feeling of joy and peace.

Everything began, he says, "to sing with strength and with conviction."

At the church, Father Ford, whom Merton had come to see, was out. Merton stepped back into the street, only to find Father Ford coming around the corner.

"Father, may I speak to you about something?"

"Yes, sure. Come into the house."[2] They sat in a little parlor by the door. And Merton said, "Father, I want to become a Catholic."

One is reminded of C. S. Lewis's observation that a young man wishing to preserve his atheism cannot be too careful of his reading.

Father Ford suggested caution. Perhaps Merton should come back in a week to ten days if he continued to feel the same. But Merton, who had been reluctant before, was now full of conviction. He insisted upon beginning his instructions at once.

Of course, this prompting of which Merton speaks did not occur in a vacuum. For some time before this, Merton had been examining Christianity in a very serious way; he had been reading; he was beginning to pray; he had already had some very real religious experiences. All the same, the prompting of which he speaks is, or can be, a very real force in the experience of conversion. An idea occurs to the convert, not vaguely or as a possibility for later action, but insistently, almost demanding to be heard. This movement of the spirit is real, it is urgent, too insistent to be put aside. To read of this in another convert's life is reassurance that one's own experience is not bizarre, unreal, or fantastic but commonplace in the life of the spirit.

This intrusion of the life of grace into the day-to-day experience of an ordinary person, this prompting which is so real, so insistent, so haunting, and at the same time so loving, this encounter with a reality beyond the ordinary experience of life, an encounter which is definite, persistent, and demanding—this is conversion.

I trust by now it will be clear that—in the context of this book at least—conversion is an inner change of heart, not an outward change of allegiances; not a matter of worshipping in one church or another; not a matter of belonging to one denomination or another. Such changes do occur in the working out of a given religious conversion. Yet it may also happen that conversion merely roots the convert more deeply in the religion to which he was born and in the church in which he was brought up. After his meeting with God in conversion, the convert may live in the same town, teach in the same university, belong to the church his father and mother attended. But at the same time a momentous awakening has taken place. "But weren't you already a Christian?" people sometimes say to me, when I speak to them of my own conversion. The answer is that I was and I wasn't. To be brought up Christian is only half the battle; indeed, for some, it is one of the obstacles along the way. Conversion is not a matter of changing religions, but of a change in oneself. The whole course of the convert's life is altered by the awakening of faith in him. A whole new life, inexorable, relentless, and invisible except to the eyes of faith—a sometimes baffling, mostly glorious process is set in motion, and the convert can say, with Paul:

> True, I am living, here and now, this mortal life, but my real life is the faith I have in the Son of God, who loved me, and gave himself for me.[3]

Evelyn Underhill, the Anglican writer and mystic, has this to say of conversion in her book entitled *Practical Mysticism:*

> Those who are so fortunate as to experience in one of its many forms the crisis which is called "conversion" are seized, as it seems to them, by some power stronger than themselves and turned perforce in the right direction. They find that this irresistible power has cleansed the windows of their homely coat of grime; and they look out, literally, upon a new heaven and a new earth. The long quiet work which others must undertake before any certitude rewards them is for these concentrated into one violent shattering and rearranging of the self, which can now begin its true career of correspondence with the reality it has perceived.[4]

While I would quarrel with Underhill's notion that this power in our lives is irresistible, for I think that God's power only works in our lives if we let it, her definition of conversion as a "violent

shattering and rearranging of the self" is an excellent beginning
point for reflections on conversion. Underhill says that, after this
rearrangement, the self can now begin its true career. This career
of "correspondence with reality" is not just an aspect of the initial
turning, it is the work of a lifetime. John McCall, a contemporary
psychologist, has said that "conversion is the essence of the Christian vocation," adding that "conversion is never once and for all,
it's a process, a continuing series of events."[5]

[margin handwritten note: to know A reality which demands a response from us]

A different and perhaps even more direct definition of what
conversion is came about in a conversation which took place between Thomas Merton and his poet friend Robert Lax, as they
walked along a New York street in the spring of 1939. Impatient
that Merton, even after his acceptance of Catholicism, still saw
his life dream as personal literary success, Lax suddenly challenged
him:

"What do you want to be, anyway?"

Covering up his real ambition to be a renowned literary critic,
Merton responded that he wanted to be "a good Catholic." But
Lax saw through his statement and offered an alternative:

"What you should say is that you want to be a saint."

Merton protested that he couldn't be a saint, that wanting to
be a saint won't make one a saint. What he really meant was that
he was afraid even to entertain the possibility.

Lax had a clearer vision in the matter: "All that is necessary to
be a saint is to want to be one. Don't you believe that God will
make you what he created you to be, if you consent to let him do
it?"[6]

So Lax expressed what Merton was only beginning to grasp:
that conversion is a kind of consent to the loving will of the Lord
in our lives, a surrender to the transforming power of his love. To
do this is to rebuke all that is willful and disobedient in ourselves,
and turn to the Lord without reservation; and only through this
turning can the old self be transformed into the new.

As we consider the many ways it happens, differently and
uniquely in each person's life, it will be useful to remind ourselves
from time to time that conversion is not a change we bring about
in ourselves but which God brings about in us. It is transforming

work, work of transfiguration. It is work which proceeds, in spite of the overwhelming power of God's love, only as we permit ourselves to be filled with that love, only to the extent that we can say: "Here I am, Lord; I come to do your will."

For to know that God lives, and loves us, is not merely to know a fact; it is to know a reality which demands a response of us, and that response is one of love. To know that the sky is blue is to know a fact (which is, as it turns out, an appearance). To know that God made us and loves us and made us to receive his love is to know something which draws us, which commands, which attracts, and which reshapes and re-forms us (reforms us!) according to our own willingness to receive love, to love, and to offer up our own wishes, preferences, prejudices, and desires, in loving obedience and adoration.

This experience of transformation is ever-present in the Christian life; conversion is not, as McCall says, a "once and for all event." Yet the Christian life, the life of grace, begins for each person some time; and that first encounter with God can be so powerful and so changing that it seems to be the decisive event of a lifetime, the event after which any other must be less, an event which shapes everything that comes after. It is this first turning which is the subject of this book; the further turning which is the ordinary business of living as a Christian will also be dealt with but only after our converts have passed through the first doorway into the Christian life.

In choosing to reflect upon my own conversion experience and several others like my own, I feel a certain hesitation, however. I do not think the reader should conclude—I do not think I can conclude—that these experiences are the only sort of conversion, or even the best sort. Both scripture and psychology tell us that there are many kinds of conversion experience.

Some are converted by visions and private revelations like Saul of Tarsus on the Damascus road. In this book there will be no such accounts. Some are converted, like the eunuch who talked with Philip, in an afternoon. The conversions of which I will write took considerably longer. Some turn to the Lord as children and never turn away again. Some turn to the Lord as children,

turn away, and then turn back. Some experience a special religious
awakening which comes in early adolescence. (Newman writes of
such an experience when he was fifteen, though his conversion in
the sense that we usually think of it came much later on.) Some
are converted—turned in their courses—by a powerful event: Peter
Marshall—walking alone on a dark night across a Northum-
berland moor—was stopped in his tracks by a voice insistently
calling his name, and prevented from falling to certain death in
an abandoned stone quarry; this incident was one of many he interpreted as God's hand in his life, leading him to give his whole
life to the Lord. Some experience a conversion which is nearly instantaneous. William James writes of several such conversions in
The Varieties of Religious Experience. I will not write of such
conversions, not because I doubt that they occur, but because they
are not within my own experience.

The conversion experience of which I will write is but one way
of conversion which has taken place with adult, educated, intellectual, twentieth-century persons, all Christians. I do not pretend
that their experience is typical. Indeed, what may be of value
about it is that it is so very particular and personal.

For a long time after my own conversion, I was reluctant to talk
about the experience. I felt eccentric and out of step with my contemporaries; it seemed to me unlikely that others could understand what had happened to me. Sometimes, when I tried to explain it to those who were already believers, they too made me
feel that I had had an experience so unusual, so idiosyncratic, that
it could not be shared.

I have learned slowly what Lewis seemed to know from the beginning: that no experience is so personal that it cannot be shared
with someone, even though one's own experience cannot always
be shared with everyone. And Lewis says that such sharing is often
the starting point of friendship: a revelation of self which brings
the response, "What, you too? I thought I was the only one."

The psychologist Carl Rogers, in his book *On Becoming a Person*, has expressed the same insight this way:

> There have been times when . . . I have expressed myself in
> ways so personal that I have felt I was expressing an attitude

which it was probable that no one else could understand. . . . In these instances I have almost invariably found that the very feeling which has seemed to me most private, most personal, and hence most incomprehensible by others, has turned out to be an expression for which there is a resonance in other people. . . .[7]

From this, Rogers develops a formula which gives me courage. He says that what is most personal is most general. I do not know whether, in the matter of religious conversion, this maxim can possibly apply, for it is so obviously an experience known to some and quite unknown to others. Nevertheless, I hope Rogers is right to this extent: that what is most personal to the conversion experience I describe will be general at least in that it is illuminating to others, whatever their course in life may be.

I think another reason for my reluctance—up to now—to write about conversion experience, especially my own, was a fear that this experience could be interpreted in strictly psychological terms. Let us take, for example, Lewis's concept of conversion as a regress—a "turning home." Isn't that subject to a strictly psychological interpretation as a need to return to the safety and security which we felt as children? In my own case, wasn't the appeal of the church's authority, which was profound for me, an aspect of my own need for a father? I feared that such interpretations would rob the experience of its validity, might make it seem less true.

Now I think otherwise. I still think that almost every event in any conversion is subject to such psychological interpretations. But I no longer think that the psychological dimension of a conversion experience invalidates that experience. The reality is that conversion takes place within us as human beings and works through our real emotional natures. But I do not think one can therefore conclude that the experience of God is a simple projection of our human needs. Also, I do not think, in order to accept conversion as a valid experience, it is necessary to find in it some element which cannot be accounted for in the natural order of things. Perhaps that is because I no longer conceive of God's grace as a bolt of lightning which strikes our lives in a clearly miraculous fashion. To those who have experienced conversion, it may seem rather like a miracle. But the miracle has taken place not through any one inexplicable event, but rather through a succession of events, all leading in a single direction. It is the collective experience of those events which assumes a miraculous character for the convert. There is no one part of the experience which cannot be explained in other ways. The promptings which Merton and Lewis and Dulles and Griffiths and I experienced—might they not have been the voices of our own longings, rather than the voice of God? The answer is, they might have been. My purpose, therefore, is not to build a case for Christian experience as "miraculous" or unexplainable in the natural order of things. I think it very probable that every event in any conversion, including my own, might be explained in simply human psychological terms. But I am less concerned than I was about exposing conversion experiences to such interpretations. The truth of them is not so much at issue here as the reality which they have for the converts themselves. To me, it seems quite probable that God communicates to us where we are and through the dimension of our own emotional development. And it seems quite characteristic of the God that I believe in that he would send to each one of us just that sort of conversion experience which most deeply satisfies our emotional needs.

Also, I have come to feel that psychology is no longer, if it ever was, an enemy of religion. Whoever expected a psychologist to deal with conversion in the manner of a theologian? To the extent that psychologists set about their work scientifically and honestly, they provide us with very good insights on conversion.

I do think it worth mentioning, however, that my own perception of conversion differs from the one set forth by William James in *The Varieties of Religious Experience*. James is perhaps the best known psychologist on conversion, and he has, on the whole, great insight. He sets about the study of conversion with an acknowledgment that his view of the experience, excluding, as it does, theological interpretation, must necessarily be a partial one. But what I find it difficult to accept in his view of conversion is that he sees it so much as an experience in which what he calls "the divided self" becomes "unified and happy." I differ with his notion that conversion is to be equated with happiness. But even more than that, I differ with his notion that some selves are divided from the outset and others unified from the beginning. James seems to equate the need for conversion with a division in the personality. Not all personalities, he suggests, are so in need of mending. Those which are experience conversion and are thereafter mended. My own insight is that we are all divided selves, all seekers after something beyond ourselves, filled with longings that we cannot always account for or explain. For some of us, conversion provides a focus for these longings in a new view of reality which is hopeful and refreshing; but this new view of things does not totally mend us in the psychological realm; and we bring with us through the experience of conversion much the same psychological disposition which we had before. To put it another way, I do not think conversion is a matter relating primarily to emotional health. Many people, through their encounter with the Lord, have experienced healing of the emotions. But others who believe in him never fully resolve their emotional difficulties. Some of the saints remained highly neurotic people throughout their lives. It seems to me, therefore, that the psychological benefits of religious conversion ought not to be exaggerated, or presented, as some apologists do, as an incentive for conversion. The appeal of conversion ought to be that it puts us in touch with reality; it is not a self-help scheme. For some, conversion may be associated with a healthier emotional life. For others, conversion may give us the strength to bear the emotional burdens we carry. But I am inclined to think of emotional rewards as a kind of fall-out from conversion, not conversion itself. ⌐Fulton Sheen, and some other writers on conversion, have claimed that it provides certitude and peace of soul. I assent to both of these claims, provided that certitude is not equated with complete freedom from doubt and that peace of soul is not equated with emotional tranquillity. Conversion is a change of heart, a recognition of the Lord and a drawing closer to him; but it does not take us completely out of the human condition nor totally alter the cast of the personality.⌐

Psychology can provide us with many insights on the experience of conversion. But, since I believe that conversion does not take place entirely in the emotional realm, I think that psychology can only deal in part with the experience of conversion. In any case, I am not going to advance any psychological theories. Nor is my purpose apologetical—to convince readers of the truth of Christianity, even though I myself believe it to be true. I am not going to offer any sociological perspectives on conversion: my approach has not been that of the sociologist, for I am less concerned about how many people have had this experience than about what it means to those who do experience it. The Lord never promised, that I know of, that all the world would be Christian; and I am not at all sure that the conversion of a whole society matters any more than the conversion of one human being. To the extent that I intrude on the realm of theology, I beg the reader's indulgence. Though my subject is life experience, theology may creep in from time to time, but I hope to keep it within bounds.

Like writers on conversion before me, I will suggest that there are stages in the conversion experience. First, there is Desire or longing; second, the Dialectic, or argumentative, reasoning phase; third, the Struggle or crisis; and finally, the Surrender. I experienced each of these movements in my own conversion; and it seems to me I see them in each of the conversion stories which influenced me. Each phase will be treated in turn.

I have chosen to call the experience of conversion a turning, not only because that word so simply renders into English the sense of the Latin *conversio* and the Greek *metanoia*, but also because it has not one but both of the meanings for conversion which I intend. There is "first conversion"—that upheaval in our minds and hearts which we resolve when we first acknowledge the Lord and give ourselves to him. That is turning in the sense of a turnabout: a reversal, a change of course. Beyond that first conversion—as many converts learn to their surprise—there is another turning which is to last our whole life long. That is turning in another sense: transformation. In *Mere Christianity*, Lewis says:

> Every time you make a choice you are turning the central part of you, the part that chooses, into something a little different from

what it was before. And taking your life as a whole, with all your innumerable choices, all your life long you are slowly turning this central thing into a creature that is in harmony with God, and with other creatures, and with itself, or else into one that is in a state of war. . . . Each of us at each moment is progressing to the one state or the other.[8]

Not every writer calls this second process by the name "conversion." Some call it sanctification, growing in holiness. This second process may be called by many names, or described (as Paul does in the Epistles) by many metaphors, but to my mind it is still conversion. So with apologies to the reader for having to remember that I will speak of turning in two senses, I will describe (not all at once, but in sequence) two forms of conversion: not as the theologian speaks, nor as the psychologist; but as one who has experienced both forms of turning and is reminded every day of my own further need for conversion.

2

Desire

Conversion begins with longing or desire, a heart's ache for something we have never quite experienced and cannot fully describe.

This longing may come in the form of a nostalgia for a time when things seemed happier, for childhood joys which are no longer. Or this longing may take the form of world weariness, a disenchantment and disappointment with the world around us. Things as they are, even the heights of worldly pleasure, are not enough. They do not satisfy.

In part, this sense of disenchantment comes not from failure but from success. It is success which disappoints us because we had so thoroughly expected it to be the crown of life. As children, we had longed for something beyond our limited day-to-day experience, for a kind of mastery and fulfillment which childhood cannot provide. As adolescents, our longing deepened and we felt nearer to the satisfactions we thought we would experience as adults. We envisioned ourselves established, admired, the center of an attentive circle of friends, and loved—perhaps most of all, loved. But when we became adults, we were surprised to find that even the fulfillments of which we dreamed can disappoint us. Success, acclaim, love, friendship, marriage—these are real joys and yet they do not satisfy us. There is still a longing within us for an unattainable thing, a dream beyond the satisfactions of day-to-day existence: a heart's desire. It is this desire, this longing, that sends us looking—but for what, for whom?

And yet this longing is nothing new, for we have known it since childhood. What is new to us as adults is the realization that adulthood and its achievements will not lay the longing to rest. For the first time we understand that the longing which we feel is for something fundamental. The longing is deeply embedded within the personality, not the personalities of some, but the personality of everyone.

Gordon Allport, in his book *The Individual and His Religion*, calls this desire "the appetite for meaning" and suggests that it is a response to the mysterious, unexplainable nature of experience. "This appetite for meaning differs from person to person," Allport says, "and owing to nature's preference for diversity, some are satiated earlier than others. Furthermore the capacities of individuals for comprehension differ, as do ability and inclination to make use of scientific explanations and poetic metaphor. No two people have identical intellectual difficulties or powers, so no two reach identical solutions."[1]

Here Allport is speaking about the thirst for knowledge and understanding, the philosophical quest for enlightenment which is often made by the simplest men and women. Indeed, the whole business of childhood is in large part one of forming a picture of the world which fits with the day-to-day experience we have. And, as C. S. Lewis says in *Surprised by Joy*, most of our most-important thinking is done before the age of fourteen. But the longing of which I am now speaking is deeper and more fundamental even than the need for intellectual inquiry and the thirst for knowledge. It is the need which every human being feels for experience of the universe, for an encounter with existence and indeed with himself, with his own inner depths, which is the heart's ache and the heart's desire.

I say that we have known this longing since childhood, that we have, as it were, brought it along with us from childhood to maturity; yet, sometimes we experience it as nostalgia for something we knew as children. Now that we are adults, we forget the frustrations and annoyances of childhood (the being told when to go to bed, being stuffed into hats and coats, being scolded and bossed and ordered about). Instead, what we remember from our childhood is the face-to-face encounter with reality, the peak experiences which sometimes occurred when we least expected them, when feeling the sun on one's eyelids, when running very fast, when chasing a butterfly.

In their autobiographies, C. S. Lewis, Bede Griffiths, and Thomas Merton all describe childhood encounters with nature which had about them a quality of the transcendent. Griffiths writes:

> It was as though I had begun to see and smell and hear for the first time. The world appeared to me as Wordsworth describes it, with "the glory and the freshness of a dream." The sight of a wild rose growing on a hedge, the scent of lime tree blossoms caught suddenly as I rode downhill on a bicycle, seemed to me like visitations from another world.[2]

Thomas Merton, in *The Seven Storey Mountain*, describes a similar moment of exaltation in the presence of natural beauty. As a five-year-old boy, Merton recalls, he was standing with his father outdoors as the sound of church bells came to them across the fields.

> Suddenly, all the birds began to sing in trees above my head, and the sound of birds singing and church bells ringing lifted up my heart with joy.

Merton called out, "Father, all the birds are in church." Then Merton asked his father why *they* were not in church and asked whether they might go to church too. "Not now," his father answered, but promised they would go another Sunday.[3]

In the first chapter of *Surprised by Joy*, C. S. Lewis describes his first experience of beauty in nature, in a toy garden which his brother had made out of twigs, moss, and flowers in the lid of a biscuit tin. "What the real garden had failed to do, the toy garden did. It made me aware of nature—not, indeed, as a storehouse of forms and colors but as something cool, dewy, fresh, exuberant." Lewis says this toy garden forever influenced his concept of Paradise. And every day, from his nursery windows, Lewis could experience another vision of the unattainable: "the Green Hills," as he called them, the Castlereagh Hills in the distance. "They taught me longing—*Sehnsucht*; made me for good or ill, and before I was six years old, a votary of the blue flower."[4]

To these nursery experiences of intense longing must be added the special encounters which Lewis had through literature with an experience which he called Joy. On reading Beatrix Potter's *Squirrel Nutkin*, Lewis discovered "what I can only describe as the Idea of Autumn," which produced in him a pleasure so intense that he returned to the book again and again to taste it. Still another such experience came through reading Longfellow's *Saga of King Olaf*, in which a certain passage so moved him that he says, "I was uplifted into huge regions of northern sky" and desired "with an almost sickening intensity something never to be described." Perhaps the most striking of all these early experiences of Sehnsucht is the one which Lewis calls "a memory of a memory." Standing beside a flowering currant bush on a summer day, Lewis suddenly has a memory of an earlier morning when his brother had brought his toy garden into the nursery. Lewis can barely find words to describe the intensity of this sensation. "Milton's 'enormous bliss' of Eden (giving the full, ancient meaning to 'enormous') comes somewhere near it." In this particular moment, Lewis senses the longing for longing which is the particular characteristic of the experience which he calls Sehnsucht or Joy. In the preface to *The Pilgrim's Regress*, he describes this experience of intense longing and distinguishes it from other longings. With other longings, there is pleasure only as long as one knows that the desire will soon be gratified. But with Joy or Sehnsucht, the longing itself, the mere wanting, without the hope of satisfaction, is experienced as pleasure and delight. And yet at the same time this wanting is acute and sometimes painful! Of this special kind of longing, Lewis says: "This hunger is better than any other fulness; this poverty better than any other wealth." It even happens that if the wanting is not felt for some time, there is a wanting of the wanting, ". . . and that new desiring becomes a new instance of the original desire. . . ."[5] Yet Lewis understands that this most desirable desire, however much we might wish to repeat it, is something that happens to us and cannot be willed by us. Lewis says of it in *Surprised by Joy:* "I doubt whether anyone who has tasted it would ever, if both were in his power, exchange it for all the pleasures of the world. But then Joy is never in our power and pleasure often is."[6]

Bede Griffiths, in describing his own schoolboy encounter with nature, says, "It came to me quite suddenly, as it were, out of the blue, and now that I look back on it, it seems to me that it was one of the decisive events of my whole life." Griffiths says that from that time on he began to experience "an overwhelming emotion in the presence of nature, especially at evening. It began to wear a kind of sacramental character for me. I approached it with a sense of almost religious awe, and in the hush which comes before sunset, I felt again the presence of an unfathomable mystery. The songs of the birds, the shape of the trees, the color of the sunset, were so many signs of this presence, which seemed to be drawing me to itself."[7]

The immediate result of this in Griffiths' life was to make him a nature worshipper or, in Lewis's phrase, "a votary of the blue flower." But for both Lewis and Griffiths this experience of joy in nature became a religion unto itself, which bore no relationship, in their thinking, to the Christian religion. Griffiths says that the first effect of such a nature experience may be the abandonment of all religion. "Wordsworth himself was to spend many years in the struggle to bring his mystical experience into union with orthodox Christianity and it may be doubted whether he was ever quite successful."[8]

And Griffiths is also aware that the sense of the transcendent, the "transforming illumination" such as he had, comes to each of us in different ways; may come

> as it came to me, through nature and poetry, or through art and music; or it may come through the adventure of flying or mountaineering or of war; or it may come simply through falling in love, or through some apparent accident, or illness, the death of a

friend, a sudden loss of fortune. Anything which breaks through the routine of life may be the bearer of this message to the soul.[9]

Griffiths thinks that not only pleasure but also pain may be the occasion for heightened or transcendent experience. And he recognizes, as Lewis does, that this moment of "grace" or Joy, this heightened experience of reality, may be lost or taken away. This loss of the mystical encounter is described in many places by Wordsworth:

> But there's a tree, of many, one
> A single field which I have looked upon,
> Both of them speak of something that is gone:
> The pansy at my feet
> Doth the same tale repeat
> Whither is fled the visionary gleam?
> Where is it now, the glory and the dream?[10]

Lewis too observed, as Griffiths did, the similarity between his own intense experience of Joy and that of loss or grief. He says that Joy, apart from the fact that it is an experience we want to repeat, might just as well be called a kind of grief or unhappiness, although it is a kind we want.

There is an example of this in Thomas Merton's conversion story. He describes the first infusion of grace into his mature life as an unexplainable encounter which took place perhaps a year after his father's death. While on a visit to Rome, alone in his hotel room with the light on, Merton suddenly thought that his dead father was present with him. This incident took place "in a flash," but in that flash Merton had a first insight, he thought, into his own sinfulness or, as he put it, into the "misery and corruption of my own soul." For the first time in his life, Merton wanted to escape from sinfulness "with an intensity and an urgency like nothing I had ever known before." Not only was this sense of his father's presence unusual to Merton, but he had no clear perception of what caused it, was reluctant to think of it as any real communication with his dead father, as he had always had an antipathy towards any form of communication with the dead. Yet in his account, Merton calls the experience "a grace, and a very great grace." There is this, at least, to support Merton's description. He experienced something in prayer which he had not previously known: contrition. The morning after that experience of his father's presence, Merton went to the Dominican church, Santa Sabina, with the firm intention to pray. "It was a very definite experience," he writes, "something that amounted to a capitulation." Though Merton was not yet a believer, had no intellectual understanding of Christianity or church teaching and would not have this knowledge for years to come, the longing, the desire, was very clear. (Later on in this same Roman visit, Merton daydreamed of becoming a monk and confided this intention to an American student friend and his mother.)[11]

On reflection, it seems to me that what each of these converts is describing (both in childhood and later on) are peak moments, moments of heightened perception in which we sense both the beauty and the power of "things"—of reality—with a special, almost painful intensity. It is an experience which is desirable but at the same time so keen that it may bring us to the verge of tears. And surely, in every life, whether in encounters with nature or with other human beings, there must be at least one and probably thousands of such experiences. Anyone who has ever known the acute mingling of pain and pleasure that constitutes first love must know what Lewis means by the longing for a longing—the desire to repeat an experience which is no experience at all but merely a dream or vision of possible joy!

But these are all recollections: "a memory of a memory beside the currant bush." However frequent such experiences are in our lives, they are mere glimpses of another kind of consciousness, a realm, as it were, in which we see and feel things more keenly and with greater intensity. We can no more hold on to or possess these experiences than we can bottle up a summer's day. They seem to be only tantalizing reminders of our mortality, of our own frailty and loneliness and need, of our finiteness and limitations.

When I was a young woman living alone for the first time in New York City, I conceived a great nostalgia for my childhood books, many of which I had not thought about for years. I bought and read again the works of A. A. Milne, the Pooh and Christopher Robin stories, and the verses: *Now We Are Six* and *When We Were Very Young*. I read again Kenneth Grahame's *The Wind in the Willows*. In fact, though I had read them before, I experienced them anew: I enjoyed Ratty and Mole and Badger in a way I think I had not done at the first reading, for as a child, one does not have the nostalgia for childhood which is the very essence of these books. So in reading these works again, I experienced something like "the memory of a memory." I did not have a name for it, but I think it was what Lewis calls Joy. I also read Lewis Carroll. I enjoyed him as I had never done on my first reading (at seven, when the Tenniel illustrations frightened me) or on my second reading (at twelve, when my real fascination was in working out the chess moves described in *Through the Looking Glass*). Looking back, as I read these books again, I saw myself as a child reading them and could begin to see what kind of child I had been. The nostalgia was a form of self-discovery. Also, I used, or tried to use, these books as a way of communicating with others, that is, with other adults I knew. In doing so I gave my newly acquired copies away, though I suspect they moldered on other people's shelves, unread. While I never experienced the pleasure of knowing that these gifts had struck a responsive chord with others, I did have the pleasure of being given, in return, books and recordings by the authors and performers who had filled similar roles in my friends' lives. In this way, I recall, I first made the acquaintance of Colette, in a small volume of meditations upon various flowers, and I tasted for the first time the bittersweet quality of her writing. I re-encountered both Noel Coward and Oscar Wilde in this way, not as "childhood" writers, but as writers who had captured in some way the sadness and world weariness of our times and of their own generations.

I reread Jane Austen (without any provocation from anybody) and this too was "the memory of a memory." In Austen I could revisit a universe in which the great issues of life turned entirely upon questions of who was in love with whom. Through Austen I relived the experience of first passion—with all its longings, hopes, and rejections. How strange it was, and yet how fitting, that I should return to a writer I thought I had outgrown (because of the narrowness of her country universe) and find in her work an enormous parable of human experience: the desperate longing for affection by those walled up in country parsonages, relishing every detail of social contact, was a perfect parallel to the walled-up isolation of young New Yorkers at crowded cocktail parties, at which one knows the other guests are strangers one may never see again. The Mr. Bingleys and Mr. Darcys of Austen's books inhabit a human circle in which behavior—even an invitation to dance—counts; and slights and compliments alike are remembered forever like flowers pressed between the pages of parsonage Bibles. Yet I was coming to see that in the rush and fury of Manhattan life, invitations, slights, and compliments counted no less than in the world of Austen's characters.

This is not to say that my only Joy had been felt in literature. Like Lewis, like Griffiths, I had felt very intensely the beauty of nature, and had even committed certain passages of Wordsworth to memory because they so truly expressed my own feelings of delight with the natural universe:

> And this prayer I make,
> Knowing that nature never did betray
> The heart that loved her; 'tis her privilege
> Through all the years of natural life, to lead
> From joy to joy; for she can so inform
> The heart that is within us, and so teach
> With natural joys, that neither evil tongues,
> Harsh judgements, nor the sneers of selfish men,
> Nor greetings where no kindness is, nor all
> The dreary intercourse of daily life
> Can e'er prevail against us, or disturb
> Our cheerful faith, that all which we behold
> Is full of blessings.[12]

Wordsworth had found no such joy in London. So in New York I learned for the first time, in losing it, how much I had loved the beauty of nature. I came for the first time to starve for the sight of a bird, a flowering bush, a tree. It was as though I had to lose these things in order to discover what they had meant to me.

I now think that in this starvation, both for the beauties of nature and those of literature, a kind of preparation was taking place. There was an emptiness growing, a hunger for consolations which are not dreams but realities. One of the great pleasures of the twentieth century is going to see good films, which sometimes carry us to the heights of beauty and help us to experience life in a heightened way. In New York I had greater access to good films than I had ever had; yet even in this experience I began to feel a kind of loss. Films, which had once led me towards reality, I thought, now seemed to be only shadows of reality. I still found meaning in them; but sometimes I felt I was looking not at reality, but at another's construct of reality: insights which did not fully touch my own.

It is quite clear to me now that the Lord was using both this longing and this sense of loss for things I had once loved as a way of bringing me to himself. These things are beautiful, I think he must have been saying, but they are not yet the thing itself. I think he used even my confusion and hopelessness as a way of leading me to himself. One of my newfound acquaintances was an aspiring writer who was given to bouts of existential gloom. Everything, he assured me, was hopelessly bleak, and there was simply no use trying. However, he managed to combine this state of depression with a very stylish mode of life. He lived at a stylishly low rent in a rather fashionable West Village house built by the renowned New York architect, Stanford White; and there he cheered himself up periodically by spending money on first editions and costly leather-bound volumes. I think, some time later, I may unconsciously have been trying to imitate him when I bought my first leather-bound volume (still the only one I own). It was The Book of Common Prayer.

I think it must have been the first copy I ever held in my hands. When I first opened it and began to read, it broke upon me with extraordinary force. There was a familiarity about it which must have come from having heard the services read aloud on various occasions. I think I first read the passage most familiar to me, the rite of Holy Matrimony. Every line of the time-hallowed English prose was as familiar as if I had known it by heart. I think perhaps I read the burial service next, and went on to Holy Baptism. Perhaps that is when I first felt my own longing to receive this precious sacrament. In reading The Book of Common Prayer, I felt also a pleasurable sense of being at one with my ancestors, many of whom I supposed had been Episcopalians since the Reformation. Certainly the more recent generations had been practicing Episcopalians until my grandmother's time. So it was easy, because of this family tradition, to feel at home with the Anglican prayer book. It was, in some sense, already my own.

The one exception to this was the Psalter. I was already so attached to the King James Psalms (some of which I knew by heart) that I could not accept a single line variation. Now I smile to think how many different translations of Creeds and Glorias I have learned, both as an Anglican, and in my years as a Roman Catholic before and after the Second Vatican Council. In my generation, the ancient formulas have been recast (it seems to me) at least a half-dozen times, and I have cheerfully memorized each new translation. But in those days I was clinging to the old texts as to a kind of revealed word; they were my way to the past I wanted to reclaim. I had, as a Southerner, been brought up with very strong notions of the importance of family heritage and tradition. Religious belief, I was now beginning to think, was part of that tradition. Perhaps that is why, when I began to consider Christianity in earnest, I had so much interest in historical arguments, both for the authenticity of the Gospels, of the letters of Paul and the other disciples, for the validity of the Church of England and the Church of Rome, for the matter of apostolic succession, the manner of receiving and celebrating the Eucharist, and the issues which arose at the Reformation over all these various forms, practices, and traditions. It may be that I gave them importance, in part, because my own family had given such importance to its own handed-down customs, stories, and personal treasures: family portraits, jewelry and china, even my great-grandmother's silver thimble. Perhaps another person, not raised in such a way, might never have related to religion this way at all. Later on, I think I began to understand Catholic attitudes about the saints because my family had such a fondness for graveyards. When we took our older relatives for drives on Sundays, they so often asked to go to the cemetery so they could visit other members of the family! So it is, I see in retrospect, that a longing to return to my own family traditions, not so much those of my mother's generation, but of generations before hers, was a very special part of my own nostalgia. I cannot say that I have found this experience mirrored in the stories of other converts. Yet this must have been nostalgia for my own childhood: for my grandmother and her sisters used to entertain me for hours telling me what life had been like when they were children and lived on the plantation.

An aspect of this nostalgia, this desire, was that I became a frequenter of churches. I did this for quite a long time without understanding it, or perceiving it as a movement towards conversion. I may in some instances have told myself that I was only visiting them because they were beautiful places, filled with lovely paintings and artifacts. But I could not have explained it this way in all cases, for in many Catholic churches I found the decor positively repellent. (Avery Dulles had this same difficulty.) I did not care for, or understand, Catholic devotional art. In the churches I had visited in Mexico, I was sometimes shocked by the literal representations I saw of the suffering Christ: there was too much blood and anguish in them for me. I was not fully comfortable with statues in any case, for as a Protestant I had come to think Catholic veneration of statues was superstitious; I especially thought that devotion to Our Lady was excessive. But during this time, I did not visit only Catholic churches; I visited churches of every denomination. In the Episcopal churches I felt most at home. There was just enough beautiful stained glass in them to give me a great deal of pleasure, and not so much that I felt overwhelmed by it. The inscriptions and carvings were invariably beautiful. I liked, too, the plain simplicity of churches and meetinghouses of revolutionary times. And the graveyards, with their stones proclaiming a clear hope of the resurrection, attracted me profoundly.

Perhaps I had come to a time in my life when my own death was becoming real to me for the first time. For, when we are quite young, we tend to think ourselves immortal. But to the extent that I could see in my fondness for graveyards a longing for immortality, I was ashamed of that longing. I recall reading a work by Julian Huxley on immortality in which he suggested that human beings, unable to face the fact of their own deaths, construct myths of survival as a defense. This seemed to me a very logical explanation of religious teachings on immortality. I could not accept religion merely as a way of consoling myself, or deceiving myself, about the fact of death. I wanted the truth, not fairy tales. Like Lewis (I was to learn later), I thought the church's teaching on immortality something of an unfair inducement. I would not become a Christian simply for that reason.

In retrospect, it seems to me that my frequenting of churches was a desire to get in touch with my own past. The three sorts of churches that most attracted me were Episcopal, Catholic, and Lutheran, these being the three branches of Christianity to which my forebears had belonged. I wanted somehow to be in touch with that. I was no longer (despite my upbringing) able to be a Christian Scientist. I had read extensively in the works of Mary Baker Eddy and though I was grateful to Christian Science for giving me some knowledge of the Scriptures and a positive and hopeful view of humanity, I could not accept its philosophical views. I was troubled by the things Mrs. Eddy had left out of her creed. She did not accept the reality of evil; and it seemed to me from observation and experience that evil was in some sense real. In particular I could not deal with her denial of the reality of the material universe; this notion did not tally with my personal experience. The philosophical difficulties which I was having with her world view had made the experience of churchgoing an impossible one for me; indeed, it had made me doubt the validity of all religion.

Looking back, it seems to me that what was most absent for me in Christian Science was most present in the Episcopal, Catholic, and Lutheran churches, namely, the concise statement of orthodox Christian belief which is found in the Apostle's Creed. In the back of my mind was the echo of a statement which had been made by the father of a friend of mine named Argyll Campbell. His father had remarked about Christianity: "If you're going to take it, take it all." I did not yet know whether I could take it; but I was beginning to see that I could not take part of it and leave the rest alone.

But this perception—that it was the creed of Catholic, Anglican, and Lutheran churches that attracted me to them—is hindsight. At the time I am speaking of, I was attracted to these churches without being able to articulate the reason. It was, quite simply, nostalgia: desire.

I think now that in my visits to churches and to churchyards I was subconsciously attempting to deal with the issue of flesh and spirit—the issue which was causing me such difficulties in Christian Science. Lewis describes himself before his conversion as a "thoroughgoing materialist," by which he means one who believes that matter is all there is. As a Christian Scientist I was asked to be a thoroughgoing spiritualist, one who believes that spirit is all there is. Humanly, I think I must have felt that the truth lay somewhere in between. (Indeed, with the help of such Christian thinkers as Teilhard de Chardin, I think that now.) Like Lewis, like Dulles, like Griffiths, like Wordsworth, I had glimpsed God in the material universe. Somehow I needed to work out a scheme which would allow for the existence of both matter and spirit.

Churches, I think, symbolized this fusion of matter and spirit. In the beauty of glass and wood and stone, they spoke of a spiritual reality made visible in the material. In them I saw a glimpse of holiness, and understood—as the Greeks did in their sacred groves—the notion of holy places, of hallowed ground.

It was this insight—which came to me then only dimly—which later was to make traditional Christianity (what Chesterton calls orthodoxy) so profoundly appealing to me. Jesus had healed by the laying on of hands. He had spat on the ground, mixed spittle with dirt, and applied it to the blind man's eyes. He had turned the water into wine; multiplied the loaves and fishes; eaten broiled fish and honeycomb after his resurrection. The apostolic succession—a priesthood passed down from one human being to another by a sacramental laying on of hands—this, too, spoke of spirit and matter as inextricably linked. Indeed all the sacraments were material things transfigured by spirit: the bread and wine of the Eucharist, the water of baptism, the oil of the final anointing. Anointing, through the centuries, had been a way of making men into kings. It was attractive to me to think that God might use his material creation to bring men and women to holiness. As I began, in my own way, to try to fit together all the pieces of history and tradition and custom and doctrine and philosophy into some sort of a mosaic which would reveal an image, there was a need to see material things—including the body—as capable of goodness.

In my visits to churches—prompted by desire—I was not yet able to articulate these questions. All I was doing was looking for myself, for my own past, for a sense of my own identity, of who I really was. In the secure world of my home city, New Orleans, I thought I had known that beyond any doubt. Once I was away from home I could see that I was a stranger, a wanderer in the universe, without a place to stand. Sartre and Camus made me feel that I would always be a stranger, that the nature of experience was such that we must always be aliens. I felt the alienation; but I felt also a strong sense that somewhere, someday, I would be at rest, at home.

One thing I did find in my roamings. I began to develop a strong sense of my own Englishness: the Englishness of my American ancestors. They were the ones—through my mother and grandmother and great-aunt—that I felt I knew best. Through generations of Americans of English descent, I felt a nostalgia for a homeland I had never seen. I did not yet know (could never have guessed!) that it was to be in great part English Christians (Lewis and Griffiths among them) who would lead me to the faith. I did not yet understand that my love for English literature was partly for the Christianity in it: in Milton and Herbert and Donne, in Wordsworth and Tennyson. Even if I had recognized this, I would not have been able to become a Christian for that reason. One of my difficulties lay in thinking that I was cut off, by the nature of modern enlightenment, from the simple faith my ancestors had.

But the nostalgia was real, and ultimately it was one of the ways in which the Lord brought me to the faith. Looking back now, it seems to me quite clear that it is through our human needs—for identity, for a sense of family, for a sense of belonging —that conversion works most naturally and most profoundly.

So, out of our human longings, out of a nostalgia for childhood joys, out of a sense of alienation from things as they are, out of disenchantment, we come at last to an understanding—some sooner, some later—that there is a desire within us for something greater than ourselves, a hunger which we ourselves can never satisfy.

To see this for the first time is to feel a sudden isolation, a sudden helplessness.

It is to know all at once that we can never provide for ourselves, under our own power, our own fulfillment. We see that we are not enough for ourselves, by ourselves; and that others—friends, wives, husbands, lovers—cannot satisfy us in that deepest part of ourselves where this heartfelt longing dwells. We know that we need something or someone, even if we cannot yet call that someone God. In fact, this new knowledge is profoundly disturbing, for we are not yet able to admit our need for God to ourselves out of a fear that he may not exist, after all.

Conversion, then, is not a disinterested intellectual pursuit. It is not a scholar's dispassionate examination of the arguments for and against deity. It is a struggle for the conquest of philosophical and historical questions which we cannot make dispassionately; for the answers—if there are answers to be found—will touch us profoundly at the deepest level of our being. Yet, to satisfy ourselves, not to delude ourselves, we must work with the sharpest tools of reason and argumentation which we have; we cannot leap over the intellectual and historical obstacles merely by wishing to.

Converts want God. In their hearts, in their very bones, they desire him. Yet this very wanting is often the greatest obstacle to believing in him. We are afraid to believe in God, afraid that it is our own need which has created him, as in Voltaire's famous remark: "If God had not existed, it would be necessary to invent him." A great many serious thinkers have raised this argument against belief. But converts themselves, who feel the longing for

God most keenly, must raise it themselves; their experience demands that they do so.

There is, of course, a converse to the argument that we have invented God because we need him. It is the argument that this desire would not exist within us were there not a corresponding object for it, somewhere in the universe. C. S. Lewis expresses it this way:

> It seemed to me therefore that if a man diligently followed this desire, pursuing the false objects until their falsity appeared and then resolutely abandoning them, he must come out at last into the clear knowledge that the human soul is made to enjoy some object that is never fully given—nay, cannot even be imagined as given—in our present mode of subjective and spatio-temporal experience. This desire was, in the soul, as the Siege Perilous in Arthur's castle, the chair in which only one could sit. And if nature makes nothing in vain, the One who can sit in this chair must exist.[13]

Lewis here suggests that the desire for God is in its way a proof for the existence of God, and hangs it on a very important supposition, namely, that nature makes nothing in vain. (Critics might say that only one who already believed in an orderly and caring Power behind the universe could make this supposition!)

However, Lewis operated on this supposition himself when working out his own faith commitment; for one of the courses he took in conversion was testing by experience whether any other form of earthly pleasure or affection could satisfy the desire which he felt within himself. He describes this process as "the dialectic of Desire." He is aware of course that this longing readily accepts false objects, at first; but he also says that "the Desire itself contains the corrective of all these errors." If followed faithfully, this dialectic would cause you to live through "a sort of ontological proof." And this way of approaching belief in the practical order Lewis called a "lived dialectic." When he pursued it, together with "the merely argued dialectic of my philosophical progress," he found that the two paths eventually converged. This convergence of the dual paths—as Chad Walsh observed in his comments on *Surprised by Joy*—is a striking feature of Lewis's conversion. And we can be confident that Lewis is accurately recounting this intellectual and intuitive convergence, for he describes it in just the same way in *The Pilgrim's Regress*, a conversion allegory which he composed some years before *Surprised by Joy*; it is there that he clearly states this notion of living out an ontological proof. Of course, the ontological argument—that God must exist because otherwise we could not conceive of him—was not Lewis's own, but came to him from Anselm. But Lewis's notion of living out an ontological proof seems to have been very much Lewis's own: part of his own particular path of conversion.

In any event, it is clear that conversion begins with a restlessness of the human heart which can find no resting place on earth. In the words of still another convert, Augustine: "You have made us for yourself, and our heart is restless until it rests in you."[14]

The desire for God is the first step towards God. Once one comes to believe in him, it is only natural to suppose that the Love which is beyond all loves would have given us a longing and desire for himself. What could be more natural than for a Lover to attract his beloved? But this understanding grows only with faith. For the inquirer, the convert who as yet has no such faith to shape his viewpoint, this new awareness of a need which nothing earthly can satisfy is not a joyful one but full of doubt and confusion. The convert's new interest may become a burden. It may haunt him with a sense of being different, neurotic, out of step. He cannot account for his new appetite for religious questions, but, try as he will, he cannot leave them alone. As much as he wants to think about God, he wants also to be rid of thinking about him. He wishes for objectivity to think the issue through, but finds himself ruled by very subjective feelings instead. Influenced, perhaps, by some psychologists, he suspects his religious longings of being the result of suppressed desires or sublimation. (This was the issue which Lewis worked out in his "lived dialectic.") But psychology is not the real obstacle. Instead converts are plagued by the argument from "common sense." It is "common sense"—a sense of the ordinary—which makes us skeptical of God's extraordinary attraction; it is suspect because it is so very perfect, so exactly what we wished for; it has about it the character of myth and make-believe, of happy endings. The convert cannot believe in God because God is too good to be true.

So an irony exists in the longings converts feel—especially intellectual converts—for God. It is one thing to feel these longings; it is quite another to consent to them. One dares not be swept away by the sheer romanticism of a beautiful myth. The demands of intellect must be met; the questions must be raised; answers must be found. The desire itself must be examined and understood: if it does not have a corresponding reality, then clearly it will be diagnosed as an ailment, an affliction caused by the frustration of some other need. An acceptable hypothesis must be found, and there seem to be only two ways to approach it: the argued dialectic of logical thought and the lived dialectic of discovering whether the desire for God can eventually be satisfied by something else instead.

3

Dialectic

I turn now to the Dialectic: the argumentative or reasoning stage of conversion. I am aware that not every convert passes through this stage. It seems possible to leap over it or pass it by (as in some instantaneous conversions) and move immediately into the stage which I call Struggle, or the crisis. But the converts who were my models did not; neither did I. There are many converts (Augustine is one) who spent a long time working away at the issues on a rational basis before they were willing to make any personal choices or take any committing steps. This process has been known, throughout Christian history, as the conversion of the intellect, and has been contrasted with the conversion of the heart. But in fact, any authentic conversion involves both the mind and the heart. In some conversions, one element is emphasized more than the other; but in authentic conversion, it is not one element of the person but the whole person—mind, heart, and will—that turns to the Lord.

This stage which I call the Dialectic is a stage of inquiry and investigation, but it is not, in the first stages at least, a conscious search for God. What the inquirer is doing is turning over every possibility and examining every hypothesis which will help him to make sense of his experience. The process seems less religious than philosophical. He or she is trying to find a clue to the meaning of the universe. At the beginning, the idea of God may seem like the least plausible solution.

The Dialectic is a dialogue, then, but not one which takes place with other persons or even one other person. The popular impression that a man or woman is "converted" by an encounter with some persuasive or charismatic person is not, to my mind, the way in which the Dialectic takes place. Instead, the Dialectic is an interior dialogue. Within the self there is a constant tension between that pole of the convert's personality which is drawn towards belief and the pole which resists it. It is true that in some conversions personal encounters have been decisive: the dialogues between Ambrose and Augustine, between Pusey and Newman, between C. S. Lewis and certain of his believing friends would be examples of this. And personal encounters between reader and author are equally influential. But one should not suppose that in such encounters one person "converts" another. Ultimately, the inquirer might be said to convert himself. His choice, when it is made, is made freely, without coercion or undue influence. Until the time when that commitment must be made, the inquirer seeks out opinions and hypotheses which bear upon and inform his own interior dialogue. These people and philosophies which the convert seeks out are many-sided. Not all are believers or belief positions; some are opposed to belief. The inquirer will not have the argument loaded or tipped in any way, but wants to hear both the atheists and the believers out to the last. For, however much, subconsciously, the inquirer may want to believe, his intellect demands that he be brought to it honestly. No less rational mode will do. He cannot fling himself blindly into the arms of the Lord; no other person's resolution of the matter will suffice; his answer, his response, must be his own entirely. The convert is not in dialogue with any man. His dialogue is within himself, a tension between his own poles of doubt and affirmation.

And the convert knows best how the argument must develop. For he knows better than anyone alive what difficulties and obstacles must be dealt with before a genuine faith experience is possible. I am often struck, in random conversations with those who doubt the existence of God, with how quickly and easily they can state the central issue which keeps them from belief: "How can there be a God when there is so much evil in the world?" "How can I believe that God is good when he is treating me so badly?" So each person is his or her own best dialectician. Perceiving best where his or her own gravest difficulties lie, each person (spurred or prompted by Desire) seeks out the sources which can best enlighten his own pockets of doubt and darkness.

For many people—especially in this century—the first and gravest obstacle is the argument from science: a view that God is inconsistent with modern enlightenment and intellectual freedom.

Avery Dulles says that in his first year at Harvard he was sure that men could no longer believe in God. It was simply inconsistent with scientific progress and the discovery of evolution. Religion, Dulles thought, was out of date: modern people could no longer take it seriously. Morality, he thought, was only "a sort of social contract expressive of the general desires of the community."[1] Dulles thought religion belonged to a superstitious past; he also thought it was a matter of feeling. He explained to an Anglo-Catholic priest he met at Harvard that he had no religious feeling and was quite comfortable as an atheist. He was quite convinced he could never develop a faith based on feeling.

But when Dulles began to study philosophy—Aristotle and Plato—he began, without knowing it, to be drawn into the dialectic of his conversion. He was impressed with the Greeks, more so than the modern philosophers. He thought they had gone farther toward "solving the problem of being."[2] This was what Dulles was trying to do; as yet he had no idea that God had anything to do with the matter. Like Lewis, like Griffiths (like a thousand thousand other seekers), he was trying to construct a rational model of existence to guide his life and thought.

Aristotle helped him to acquire a deeper understanding of the material universe, to recognize "that things are something more than hard atoms or bouncing electrons . . ." to let go of his view that the material is the real . . . and then "to understand how the Supreme Being, as 'Pure Act,' impassable and immutable, might

be altogether immaterial, and how the spiritual soul, the 'inform-
ing principle' in man, might be capable of subsisting apart from
its material partner, the body."[3] Dulles was not yet able to believe
either in God or in the life of the spirit; but Aristotle helped him
to conceive of these things for the first time. He also learned from
Aristotle, he says, to "respect final causes"—another Aristotelian
way to a concept of God. But perhaps the most important change
which Aristotle brought about in his thinking was to teach Dulles
to respect his own reason and the ability of the intellect to know
and understand reality. Dulles had been troubled by the notion
that all experience is subjective and distorted by subjectiveness.
"Aristotle convinced me," he says, "that the outer world was not
so unattainable to the senses and the mind."[4]

Without realizing it, Dulles, in accepting this insight of Aristotle's, had taken the first step in the reasoning process which was to
lead him at last to faith. He had come, through the reading of a
non-Christian philosopher, to trust the use of his own reason as a
way of discovering reality. Up to that point, Dulles's world view
had been confining, discouraging, confusing. Believing in nothing
beyond himself, and not very much in himself, trusting little in
the power of his own mind to come to grips with reality, he found
little to be hopeful about. But this new insight from Aristotle was
liberating. "I all at once felt at home in the universe," he writes.
"It is impossible for me to exaggerate the sense of joy and freedom I felt [on discovering the dignity of reason]. . . ."[5]

He found next in Plato an answer to another serious difficulty
of his: that morality is simply the projection of the particular
value systems of certain groups in society. Because of this belief,
Dulles had found morality unattractive, for who would want to
abide by the moral constraints of any particular subgroup? "I
could see nothing noble and inspiring in making oneself a pliant
instrument of the aspirations of others. . . ."[6]

But Plato led him to believe in Virtue by first confirming what
Dulles already believed about Beauty. "In my esthetic theories
. . . I was already half a Platonist." Dulles had already rejected
the argument that beauty is entirely in the beholder's mind, that a
thing might be esthetically indifferent: beautiful to one person

and ugly to another. "The artist, I observed, aimed . . . to embody in lasting form the ideal which, by a mysterious process, sprang up within his soul."[7] On becoming acquainted with Plato's idea of the Good, Dulles immediately associated it with his own idea of Beauty. But Plato's Good, unlike Dulles's Beauty, "was transposed to the higher plane of the invisible."[8]

So, in very short order, Dulles, through his reading of Plato, began to accept the moral law and the necessity of virtue, so far, by his own account, without having seriously considered a single Christian thinker. What he had done (which seems to be characteristic of some other intellectual conversions as well) was to place the ancient thinkers and the modern ones on an equal plane and weigh their ideas according to their own rational appeals to him rather than according to the value system—which Lewis calls "chronological snobbery"—which places modern ideas on a higher plane than ancient ones. The ideas which Dulles was finding in Plato and Aristotle he accepted, not because they were current or fashionable, but because they matched his own view of reality and experience. He accepted them not on the authority of others but because they rang true. And, presumably, he did not find in these ideas anything which he could not reconcile with science. They presented a scheme of reality which did not clash with modern enlightenment.

So, in his reading of only two philosophers, Plato and Aristotle, Dulles resolved "the modern difficulty." And it was entirely through the use of reason that he resolved it. His next philosophers were to be men of his own time who were in the Aristotelian tradition, the neo-Thomists Maritain and Gilson. Shortly thereafter, through a Christian teacher of literature, Paul Doolin, Dulles was to encounter the thought of Thomas and Augustine even more directly. Doolin was a convert to Christianity. What Dulles identified with most strongly in him was his Platonism, for Doolin was a Platonist, and "more than that—an Augustinian," Dulles says. "Doolin's profound grasp and appreciation of the Platonic doctrine of love was, like so many of his intuitions, based on his individual experience. His own approach to Christianity had undoubtedly been wrought with love," Dulles says, "as I suspect is the case with all conversions."[9]

So, by the reading of only a few authors in the tradition of Plato and Aristotle, Dulles had already begun to move intellectually towards God in the line of thought he was taking. And it is clear that he was doing so not because he admired a given teacher, or because it was fashionable in the circles in which he moved; indeed, in intellectually fashionable circles these lines of reasoning were considered sadly out of date. Dulles accepted them, not because of any weight of authority from without, but because he perceived an authority in them from within, one which coincided with his own reflections on reality and experience. Admittedly, the Dialectic, even after these considerable choices on Dulles's part, was barely beginning. For it is a long way from the philosophical concept of the Good and the moral imperative of Virtue to the Incarnation of Jesus Christ and the action of God revealing himself in history. Avery Dulles still had a long course of thought before him. Yet it is worth noting that it was reason, not sentiment, feeling, or even intuition, which took him over the first hurdle—the hurdle which is for many moderns an insuperable barrier to faith.

The philosophical progress which Bede Griffiths records is very close to that of Dulles (and Merton) in that he was so much influenced by Platonic thought. But Griffiths does not seem so much to need to discover God's existence through reason as to reconcile the God which can be known by reason with his own experience.

Griffiths began the formal study of philosophy with Descartes and went on to Spinoza in whom he found a philosopher "after my own heart." What he liked in Spinoza was the love of wisdom, which he had already admired in his informal reading of Socrates. For both thinkers, the pursuit of wisdom was the highest goal of a man's life. And Griffiths responded favorably to what he calls the "moral earnestness" of Spinoza. But what interested him most was Spinoza's concept of the "intellectual love of God"; Griffiths was excited to think that the "reason of the universe" could not only be known but also loved. To achieve happiness, then, a man must learn to accept the order of the universe, the "law of absolute necessity"; and men were free to choose only whether they would obey that law willingly or unwillingly. To some, such a concept of the universe might seem harsh or forbidding, Griffiths says, but for him at that moment it was reasonable and satisfying.

In all his reading of philosophy, Griffiths seems to respond most strongly not to conceptions of God or efforts to prove his existence but rather to the thoughts of philosophers on how man might respond to God within the universe. In Marcus Aurelius he admired what he calls his "piety" and deep reverence for nature. These insights were simply rational validations of Griffiths' already formed beliefs. And he says all philosophical inquiry must be so, for we can only accept what is in accord with our own lived and felt experience. But when he read Berkeley he went beyond what he already believed and took another step: seeing God as mind and the universe as the thought of that mind. In his reading of Kant, Griffiths readily accepted the distinction between the "phenomenal world" (of the senses) and the "noumenal world" (of the understanding) but could not accept Kant's view that knowledge is so affected by the structure of our own minds that it cannot bring us to reality.

What I identified with in these parallel experiences of Dulles and Griffiths was not their encounter with the philosophers they read; for either I had not read the same philosophers, or if I had read them, I had not shared their encounter with those particular minds. What appealed to me most strongly was their growing realization that thought could be trusted as a way of discovering reality.

Up to that time, I had been thinking of philosophy and literature as intellectual exercises, enjoyable and stimulating in their way, but not as a way of discovering the truth of experience. Like Dulles, I did not trust my own powers of knowing; I imagined my own thought processes so flawed by subjectivity that they could not lead me anywhere. I saw, in reading both their conversion stories, that they, too, had experienced this same difficulty. And the moment I could call it a "difficulty" it was no longer a difficulty after all.

And I identified with their gift of arriving at conclusions through literature as well as through philosophy. Up to that point in my life, I had searched literature as a way to truth; but I did not understand what I was doing. Literature, I knew, was a way of finding illumination, satisfaction, pleasure, and amusement; now I began to see that for me, and for others, it was much more.

Griffiths, for example, was strongly influenced in his philosophical progress by Coleridge. In Coleridge, as well as in Berkeley, he began to see that the God of reason, God as mind, was somehow related to the God of Christian belief. Up to this point, the idea of the Christian church and of its doctrine had hardly entered into any of Griffiths' thought about God. In Coleridge, too, he began to see the poet and the philosopher as differing mirrors of the same reality: Coleridge was both a philosopher and a poet. This insight began to help him with his own striving to reconcile reason and imagination. In all his reading, Griffiths says, he was seeking for "rational evidence for the existence of that which I had experienced in the presence of nature at school and at Oxford"—that is, the sense of the transcendent, the mystical encounter with nature and its accompanying sense of awe and wonder.[10] So Griffiths, like Dulles, accepted from the philosophers and the poets what seemed to him to clarify and explain his own experience. In their reading, both Dulles and Griffiths were seeking, not a new view of reality, but to give shape and substance to the half-formed insights which had already come to them through experience.

Griffiths, Merton, and Dulles all record with some precision the specific thinkers who influenced them (it is interesting how much they were attracted by the same ones); and they give credit both to poets and philosophers for leading them along in an intellectual progress, dealing first with the existence of God as cause, as mind, and of the universe and day-to-day experience as thoughts and influences of that Mind; with the necessity of virtue and leading a moral life; and finally, with questions of love and conformity to the guiding will of the universe.

C. S. Lewis, on the other hand, whose reading one would naturally suppose was as wide as theirs, gives us only the highlights of his reading—glossing over with such phrases as "the Christians," "the nineteenth-century rationalists," "the atheists," and so forth, what must have represented a good deal of reading from many sources. (Griffiths mentions several books which he and Lewis both read and which Lewis does not mention!) The books which Lewis does mention were those which had a decisive influence upon him. And these books show what a totally other kind of difficulty Lewis was wrestling with than that of Griffiths and Dulles with their need for a rational construct of the universe.

For Lewis, it seems, the central issue was not the possibility of God's reality or existence (though this was part of the issue) but instead with the question of what kind of force one might be called upon to deal with if one entertained the possibility of the invisible universe. Lewis's difficulties, his troubling questions, had to do with a phenomenon which I must call, for lack of a better term, Myth. From childhood upwards Lewis had an unusually rich imaginative life, and it is clear that for him imagination was something of a mixed blessing. His enjoyment both of literature and of nature from his earliest years was associated with the gods and goblins of legend; in his school years he was troubled with night fears and strongly influenced by at least one adult who believed in magic. In myths, moreover, he found personified not only good supernatural forces but also evil ones. And what seemed to haunt Lewis was not that he found it difficult to believe in the supernatural, but that he found it easy and somewhat frightening.

It is perhaps for this psychological reason that Lewis fled into atheism. He says that when he began, as a young man, to find it possible to believe in a universe without God, it was a profound relief. Mortality—which meant being freed by death of imagination and experience—struck Lewis as a welcome possibility. It was immortality that frightened him. The terror of the Christian universe, he says, was that it had "no door marked Exit."[11] So he felt comfortable with what he calls Materialism, and somewhat justified in holding that view, because it seemed both reasonable and intellectually respectable. Yet Lewis could not rest as a Materialist. He found little emotional sympathy with others holding similar views, whose energies were spent in dreams of a reformed social order and designs for political systems to bring about human happiness on earth. Instead, his heart lay with the world of imagination as he experienced it in literature. But his joy in it was only joy insofar as he was able to think it merely a matter of fiction and invention.

So, for Lewis, the question turned upon the visible and the invisible universe, and was deeply influenced by his own psychological disposition. Intellectually, he seems to have examined the arguments for and against God rather carefully, and to have determined that—in accord with the use of reason—one might hold an atheist's, an agnostic's, or a believer's view with equal intellectual consistency. Certainly he respected both the ancient and medieval philosophers whose world schemes rested upon law and order. But Lewis in his imaginative, intuitive faculty sensed another power afoot in the universe. To disbelieve in God meant that he could disbelieve in that power as well. Yet he could not entirely hold that power at arm's length, for he himself had sensed what he calls in one place the "numinous"—what the ancients described when they sensed the presence of gods and spirits in sacred groves, on prophetic islands, on holy mountains, and in underground rivers and springs.

So it was that Lewis—having relegated these "otherworldly" experiences to literature and his own world of imagination, and having carefully segregated them from his serious intellectually held positions—was shaken when he came for the first time—and this through reading Yeats and Maeterlinck—to a realization that there were other minds who gave complete credence to an invisible universe; and their supernaturalist views were held without any belief in Christian orthodoxy or even in the existence of God.

It was startling to Lewis to learn (not only through Yeats's poetry, but through his prose) that Yeats believed in a spirit world and even that contact was possible between such a world and ourselves. "To put it quite plainly," Lewis says, "he believed seriously in Magic."[12] In those days Lewis regarded Yeats as a "responsible writer," different from the spiritualists he had previously encountered. Maeterlinck, too, he thought responsible. But what really seems to have unnerved him is not so much that both writers held such views, but that they held them without being Christians. They had come to their opinions by another way, and one rather like Lewis's own: insight and experience.

What seems to have happened to Lewis then is what happens to all of us when some cherished notion or opinion on which we have been unknowingly pinning all our hopes and sense of security is toppled. He became enormously confused, one might almost say fearful. Yet the sense of danger, which he felt at the possibility of living in a world which might have not an imaginary but a real spiritual dimension, was also most exhilarating.

When this particular veil was rent, Lewis found himself able to entertain both the supernatural and the preternatural. The occult, with its admixture of evil, had always held for him a real fascination. Lewis was honest enough, even at this moment, to see that there was a good measure of nursery fear at work in his consideration of these things. And he thinks it probable that at this turning in the road he might well have veered off into Satanism or spiritualism. But at the same time his recollections of the Joy which he had experienced—Joy in his own early mystical encounters with the spiritual dimension of things—helped him to know that in the invisible world the possibility for good and beauty was at least equal to, if not greater than, the possibility for wickedness and mischief. At this one of many crises in his own dialectical progress, Lewis encountered the writer who was to carry him "across the border": George MacDonald. In reading *Phantastes, a Faerie Romance*, Lewis encountered a new idea, one that he could not give a name to. The idea was—Lewis capitalizes it—Holiness. Without his knowing it, in reading *Phantastes*, Lewis had already entered a Christian universe. In it he found a new perception— Lewis calls it a "bright shadow"—of something large enough to include the invisible universe, virtue and heroism, goodness itself. It was what he so often admired in persons who attracted him and in the authors he already loved. And because it was already familiar to him in them, Lewis says that at first he did not understand how new his perception was. But there was a difference: "For the first time the song of the sirens sounded like my mother or my nurse." Now for the first time Joy—the great passionate adventure of his life—could be seen as something akin to homely goodness and simplicity. "It was as though the voice which had called me from the world's end were now speaking at my side." Now for the first time he could begin to believe that what he had always been seeking was not imaginary but real; and that, without his knowing it, it had been with him all along. "That night my imagination was, in a certain sense, baptized; the rest of me, not unnaturally, took longer."[13]

It may seem strange to include as part of the Dialectic of Lewis's conversion an experience which is so apparently intuitive in nature and which Lewis himself can only describe in highly colored imaginative terms. But the fact is that the encounter which Lewis made through non-philosophical writers—Yeats, Spenser, Malory, and MacDonald among them—is with an idea, one which he had not previously been able to conceive of: The idea is holiness—and Lewis himself, even in his passionate description of it, calls it an idea. This idea of holiness is one which he might have found in Plato under a different name: virtue. Perhaps the ideas appear to be two, not one. But that may be because, through usage, virtue has come, in the English language, to sound like a tiresome business of refraining from everything pleasant and enjoyable in behalf of Puritanical self-denial. In the Latin, *virtus* is closely related to the word for man (*vir*) and to the word for strength (*vis*) and has about it the connotation of courage and heroism and power. So, too, does the idea of holiness as Lewis came to see it through his reading of *Phantastes*. But holiness is something beyond virtue, for it has about it a quality of the fiercely erotic and passionate: it is goodness which glows and burns, kindled by the fire of aspiration and love. Lewis perceived that holiness (though he encountered it first in myth) is not a metaphor, nor a figure of speech, nor an invention. It is a reality, an entity, a *thing*, which defines and encompasses the human encounter with the world beyond the material, with the universe itself, with a corresponding fire in others, and the joy which human beings experience in this encounter.

So a critical point in the Dialectic occurred for Lewis, when through his intellect he recognized as real something which he had previously thought imaginary: the life of the spirit in men. Until that moment Lewis could stand at the border of the Christian universe admiring the vision of Dante and the philosophy of Anselm and the doctrinal brilliance of Augustine. After that he was caught up in an inexorable process which required him to take Christianity seriously—a process which was not to be resolved for a long time.

We are accustomed to think of dialectic as an orderly reasoning process, somewhat dispassionate in nature. The Dialectic of conversion is not so. These few instances of encounters with philosophical ideas and concepts by tough, curious minds illustrate that the Dialectic—of conversion, and perhaps all dialectic on issues of substance—does not proceed in a smooth continuous movement but goes instead in fits and starts of insight and illumination. This is not to say that the process is any less reasonable. What seems to happen is that a number of ideas and arguments are collected from various sources; the mind works away at them; then, sometimes in a sudden burst of energy, a sorting and ordering occurs not sequentially, but all at once. Things fall into patterns. Even before the last piece is fitted into the jigsaw, the picture of the mountain can be seen taking shape. Then, with exhilaration, the mind rushes to complete the picture. Also, the reasoning process of the convert's Dialectic has something in common with that mental process called free association; for the puzzle, or riddle, to the solved is not one that can be guessed immediately, but one that has to be thought over and turned over, looked at from every angle, before a solution suggests itself. Then, as in a guessing game, a hint is given, a clue or lead which suggests a solution, and the mind works furiously to piece together a framework or a conclusion.

Such an illumination came to Avery Dulles, quite "suddenly and unexpectedly," after an afternoon spent reading in the Widener library. He had been poring over a chapter in Augustine's *The City of God,* assigned reading in a course on medieval history. "On an impulse I closed the book," he says. "I was irresistibly prompted to go out into the open air." He walked along the Charles River until his attention was caught by a young tree:

"something impelled me," he says. The thought came to him then
that the budding tree, in its growth and development, was following "a rule, a law of which I as yet knew nothing." This thought
provoked a question: "How could it be, I asked, that this delicate
tree sprang up and developed and that all the enormous complexity of its cellular operations combined together to make it grow
erectly and bring forth leaves and blossoms?"[14]

Dulles already had an answer in his mind, which he calls "the
trite answer of scholastic thought." Yet for him, at that moment,
the answer was totally new and fresh: that the growth of the tree
was "ordered to an end by the only power in the universe capable
of adapting needs to ends—intelligence—and that the very fact
that this intelligence worked toward an end implied purposiveness
—in other words, a will." All at once, Dulles was no longer willing
to call the force behind the universe "a mysterious force called nature." This force was intelligent; it was intelligence itself, a force
possessing both intellect and will, which, he then thought (taking
another step) combine to make personality. "Mind, then, not matter, was the origin of all things. Or rather not so much the 'mind'
of Anaxagoras as of a Person of whom I had had no previous intuition." With this additional step, Dulles saw God not only as the
original cause of the universe but as its continuing cause, a power
which (in Wordsworth's phrase) "rolls through all things." His vision of God grew; it became at least as large as the universe:

> The harmonious motions of the stars, the distribution of the ele-
> ments, and the obedience of matter to fixed laws were manifes-
> tations of the same will and plan. Looking, then, into myself, I
> beheld energies coursing through the human person. . . .[15]

He was then able to see these energies, too, as God's energy, and
thought for the first time that it was "monstrous" for human
beings to divert these energies within themselves—which they
themselves had not created—from the purpose which God intended for them. Influenced by Plato and Aristotle, Dulles saw
the soul moving naturally towards truth and goodness, and felt
that to turn it aside from this natural reaching towards goodness

was to violate the sacred order of things—to break some invisible but knowable rule or law.

So in a brief moment—standing beside a tree on the rainy bank of the Charles—Dulles was able to integrate into one vision of reality much that he had already absorbed from the ancient philosophers—Anaxagoras, Plato, Aristotle—and from later thinkers, Augustine among them. But this moment of insight was rationally based; it came about after Dulles had been engaged for some time in the dialectical process; now it became possible for Dulles to "see"—in a whole, clear vision—what till then he had only been thinking about.

Believers would say that this moment beside the tree was a moment of grace for Dulles. And the language which he uses to describe the incident suggests some sort of powerful intervention into his life at that moment. What sent him out of the library then? What "impelled" him to stop by the tree? Dulles writes of this experience as though he were somehow led. But it is not necessary to bring in grace in order to account for Dulles's thought; reason alone has led many to the same insight without trees, without rainy afternoons, without riverbanks. It was the disposition of his mind, its openness, which made the insight possible. It was his yearning that stirred the working of his mind and moved him towards the drawing of conclusions. What followed upon his reasoning is far more significant—and much more a movement of the spirit than of the mind. "As I turned home that evening," he says, "I was conscious that I had discovered something which would introduce me to a new life, set off by a sharp hiatus from the past."[16]

That night Dulles prayed for the first time in many years. He had forgotten how to pray, but it came back to him: "I knelt down in the chill blackness at my bedside, as my mother had taught me to do when I was a little boy. . . ." He recited the Lord's Prayer. "The words came slowly, and I had to make many false starts before the whole prayer unfolded itself in my mind."[17]

Dulles had made a significant crossing in one day. But it was not his intellectual recognition of God which was the decisive event. Instead, it was his response to that recognition, a response that went beyond conceptual thought and expressed itself in prayer. Many a person who comes to know, intellectually, that God is there may wait long months and years before he comes to this act of simple adoration and begins "a new life, set off by a sharp hiatus from the past."

But I do not mean to suggest that Dulles's prayer marked the end of his conversion dialectic. To pray is not always to be resolved, to be converted. Prayer may occur in any stage of conversion—as an aspect of Desire, within the Dialectic, in the Struggle, and so on. There are some who cannot pray until every stone is turned and every obstacle crossed. But with all of us, it is not so. In every life there may be moments of prayer which spring from blind panic or desperation or which flow as almost inadvertent responses to moments of pleasure or contentment. To pray at these moments may be good; but it is not the full assent, the full giving of one's heart to the Lord. In fact, prayer may be the mark not of a conviction but a wish: an aspect only of the first longings of conversion. To experience religious longings is to feel a prompting; it is not yet the real choosing which is the mark of authentic conversion.

My own Dialectic began at a time in my life when I had already experienced religion acutely and strongly. In this I identify somewhat with the experience of Dorothy Day. As a child she loved the Bible and singing hymns; she was attracted by the example of prayerful people. I had the same sweet, satisfying childhood experience in religion (an experience which Lewis, Dulles, and Merton apparently did not have). I had loved the Bible, especially the Old Testament and the Psalms. Stories like that of Jacob's encounter with the angel moved me profoundly, as did Samuel's encounter with the Lord in the temple.

Yet, even as a child, I had been troubled by the question of miraculous events such as the Virgin Birth and the crossing of the Red Sea. I did not know whether it was necessary to take them literally or whether they might be part of a mythology which existed side by side with "what really happened" to the Hebrews of ancient times. But the experience of Samuel, of David, of Daniel and Elijah all seemed quite powerful and real to me. The witness of the Hebrews to the power of God seemed to me remarkable. And my religion was one of thanksgiving and praise: I loved to sing hymns and I often felt in the beauty of nature that God was really there.

This sense of the reality of God was something which seemed to pass as I grew older. Especially in my college years, I experienced deepening and growing doubts. Was religion only a myth which had sustained our more primitive ancestors—one which modern people had outgrown? Though I had loved the Bible, I began to think of Scripture mostly as literature: an accretion of rich myths and stories no more valid than those of the Greeks, the Romans, and the American Indians. I had become interested in myths. I thought I could see definite resemblances between the myths of other cultures and the Christian stories. I think I must have read some of Frazer's *Golden Bough*, and I am certain that I read part of Robert Graves's *The White Goddess*. It seemed reasonable to think of Christianity and Judaism in the same light as the mythologies of other cultures.

Philosophy—which had been such a beginning point for Dulles and Merton and Griffiths—was for me no help at all. The study of philosophy—which, admittedly, I studied very little—seemed to me a historical succession of conflicting hypotheses, each with severe human limitations. Each philosopher's work seemed to overturn the theories which had gone before. I did not feel that I was in the presence of truth, or even getting warm. In philosophy, there was no resting place to be found. No teaching rang for me with the force of conviction or authority.

At this time in my life, I felt that I had not ever known any intelligent, well-educated people who had developed any strong intellectual basis for their faith. The only intellectuals I had ever known who were also believers were Roman Catholics, and of these I had known very few. I think I had the impression then that educated Catholics were intelligent and rational about a great many things, but religion was not one of them: where faith was concerned, they were somehow crippled by childhood religious indoctrination. In any event, the views they held about religion seemed to me rather outlandish. They belonged, I thought, to another place and time. And many Catholics I knew in college were struggling desperately with their own religious upbringing; they often seemed as troubled and uncertain as I was. To be sure, I knew a few students of philosophy who were periodically infected with a strong attraction to the Roman Catholic Church. But they managed to resist it. And when I talked with Catholics, I often found them more preoccupied with issues of personal morality (fulfillment of obligations and obedience to the Church's commands) and personal salvation (fear of hell) than with any of the questions which were troubling to me. They seemed to accept the things which I found hardest to accept—miracle, Jesus as God—without the slightest qualm. I could not enter into dialogue with them; we were too far apart.

In general, my impression about my own contemporaries was that religious people were not people of thought, and that people of thought were not religious.

Also, it seemed to me that many people were clinging to religion out of emotional needs, clinging to childhood ways of thinking. All these impressions combined to make me suspect that humanity—intellectually, at least—had outgrown religion: that it was a vestige of the simple childhood of the human race, one which in our maturity, we had to set aside.

I think, looking back, that this stage in my thinking is not uncommon with young people. For those who are raised in the faith, who have the whole of it given to them in their school years, there is nevertheless a time of testing and doubt which comes with maturation; and this crossing point provides a definite moment when some turn to and some turn away from the Lord. And there is another issue which arises at this time. There are many who call themselves Christians, who are devout churchgoers, attentive to all the externals of religion, whose hearts do not seem to bear the love which is Jesus Christ. For the lack of finding Christian love among Christians, some young people, talking angrily of hypocrisy, assume that the failures of Christians invalidate the truth of Christ.

A very strong expression of this is found in the conversion experience of Dorothy Day. Unlike the other modern converts I have mentioned, Dorothy Day had had a strong and meaningful childhood experience in religion. She had particularly identified with the prayer-lives of Catholics and with Catholic spirituality in general. From childhood friends she had learned about the saints and had found their courage and heroism inspiring. It would seem that she was already committed to the Lord. Yet in adolescence she quite definitively turned away from religion. She describes this as a conscious movement, a choice. She did not simply drift away from religious experience. She shook loose from it and turned away.

Her reasons for doing this had much to do with the downtrodden poor and suffering people of the world, with whom she so strongly identified. She did not find in the Christians she knew any strong identification with the needs of the poor and abandoned. She felt, too, that many churchgoing people were using religion as a consolation, a comfort to themselves, while manifesting a profound indifference to the needs of others. In this frame of mind, the Marxist view of religion as a drug, an opiate, to prevent the people from becoming truly aroused in behalf of their legitimate needs, was profoundly appealing. Because she could not see Christ in the Christians she knew, she rejected him outright—at least for a time. But ultimately it was this very commitment to the sufferings of others and to the needs of others which was to bring her round full circle to an encounter with God.

There is a parallel here, I think, to the experience of C. S. Lewis. However great the differences between Lewis the intellectual and Dorothy Day the servant of the poor, it seems to me quite plain that each of them fled into belief systems of some size and scope—one might almost say grandeur—as a way of avoiding the direct confrontation with the Lord to which their inner longings were calling them. Lewis, by his own admission, was afraid of such a meeting. Dorothy Day, it seems, was fed up with the Lord —I think many of us feel that at some times—for permitting so much ugliness and evil in the world and for allowing human hearts to slumber in the face of injustice and wrong.

For Dorothy Day the issues were less apparently intellectual than with Lewis. But it is possible that with Lewis the issues were also less intellectual than he made them out to be. In fact it is possible to use the intellect—and especially a nimble one—as a defense against certain realities which are troubling to us. One senses that with Lewis there was for a long time a very good intellectual grasp of reasonable ways to at least a concept of God; but his intellect, by dwelling upon difficulties and fine points of argument, deferred the inward confrontation. To put it another way, Lewis was in dialogue with God even before he believed in him. He says of this that he was angry at God for not existing; and he was also angry with him for making a world.

Dorothy Day's dialectic was like that. Her rejection of God sprang, not from a failure to believe in him, so much as from an anger at the world he had made and at the desolation in which he had left so many of his people. Such a dialectic may not resemble the cool dialectic of two philosophers exchanging views on a solution to the problem of Being. Yet, in her own way, Dorothy Day was struggling with the problem of Being in a ferociously committed and human way.

The issue in my own case lay just as deep as it did with Day and Lewis, but it was of a very different kind. I cannot say that I ever rejected God or consciously embraced any belief system which excluded him. My thoughts about God were not nearly so focused as that. If anything, I simply lost any sense of his reality, and when I did so, I did not do so in any conscious part of myself. Perhaps what I felt was a kind of isolation—a sense that God, if there was a God, could not possibly care or be concerned about me. (Indeed, this is my besetting spiritual problem to this day.)

On the other hand, I was not an atheist. The insight which Dulles had beside the tree—of an intelligent force guiding the universe, the stars and the planets, the growth of living things—was still a part of my own vision of the world. The first line of Dylan Thomas's poem summarizes what I then believed in: "the force that through the green fuse drives the flower." I had seen a power at work in the natural order and I could not forget that. That power seemed to me to have purpose and direction, to be an intelligence guiding "all things." But this view of God was of something more like a law of physics or a mathematical principle. I had been taught, in Christian Science, to believe that God is Love, but at this time in my life that statement held little meaning for me. And I was haunted by another teaching in Christian Science, a line from the chapter on prayer in *Science and Health*: "Who would stand before a blackboard and pray the principle of mathematics to solve the problem?"[18] In a way far different from what Mary Baker Eddy had intended, I interpreted that line of prose to mean that God was as unapproachable as the Second Law of Thermodynamics. I did not think (very often) of praying to a Principle. God as Principle was too abstract, too lofty and distant to be dealt with by the likes of me. And though I say that I believed in God as Principle, I am not sure that I believed in this God every day. I think I had not begun to believe, in the Christian sense, at all. I could think of God; I could conceive of him somewhat at some times. But there were long spells when I believed in nothing, when the selfishness and conflict of human behavior depressed me profoundly, and there was an emptiness in my consciousness where the notion of God might have been. He was the Being that might have focused all my confused perceptions of experience, but without faith I could not know him. Though I could sometimes think about him, I could not find him. Even the word "faith" was not fully part of my vocabulary. I heard people say joking things about "the faith"—about having it and keeping it—but did not know precisely what they meant by that word.

Oddly enough, I think my religious inquiry was given new impetus by something which took the last shred of my childhood beliefs away.

I saw a film which exploded—as I then thought—one of the key pieces of "evidence" I had been cherishing as a proof for the existence of God. The film was based on a book by a contemporary astronomer, Harlow Shapley, called *Of Stars and Men*. It dealt with the nature of the universe—space, time, energy, and motion. In the context of what I now believe, there was nothing in the film to threaten faith. It showed, with great beauty and power, the complexity, as it were, the "genius" of the universe. But in viewing the film, I learned for the first time that scientists were now able to "create" amino acids in the laboratory, converting inanimate into animate matter through the use of electricity. Until that moment I did not know how much I had been cherishing the idea that the origin of life on our planet was unexplained, even unexplainable. Now, it appeared, that a casual bolt of lightning had set off the whole process of evolution. Suddenly I felt as foolish as the nineteenth-century believers who had found Darwin threatening. What a naive construct I had been clinging to! I knew that I needed a better cosmology, one which could not be overthrown by each new scientific advance.

What I found even more unsettling about the book and the film was that Harlow Shapley himself was a believer! Somehow I felt humbled by that. I even felt a kind of envy. This was a feeling I often had, a competitiveness which rose up in me when I came upon others who could make concrete and public assertions of faith: "What does he know that I don't know? How on earth can he say that so easily?" I coveted that clarity of mind, that confidence. It seemed to me desirable, but elusive.

So for me there were really two issues intertwined: the question of whether contemporary people might believe in God; and the question of whether any genuine relationship was possible between God and man. These two questions led me—not all at once, but in a gradual process—to focus on the question of Jesus Christ. It seemed to me that he was in some ways a bridge between God and us, a ladder from earth to heaven. But was this only a poetic idea, a metaphor from sixteenth-century verse? I wanted to know who Jesus was, what he actually said and did that made people willing to die for his sake. And I wanted to know what contemporary people thought about this, for I thought I could not trust the ancients on this point, any more than one could accept the theory of the humors or hold that the sun traveled daily around the earth.

So my own starting point in the Dialectic was the issue of whether one might believe—on any decent intellectual basis—that God had acted in history and that Jesus was in any real sense his son. Revelation was the critical question. Because of this, I turned, on the whole, to sources which might enlighten me about the Scriptures: their authenticity and reliability as guides to the historical person of Christ. I came to this out of a tradition—Christian Science—which accepted the Bible fully, according to its own interpretation. In particular, Christian Scientists give unswerving belief to Jesus Christ as healer and to the actuality of his Resurrection. But because they hold a very different theology than the orthodox Christian one, I had never been taught some other articles of the Creeds: the Incarnation and the Trinity. Christian Science, I now think, is a unitarian faith, though there are vestiges of trinitarian language in it. So in my examination of the Scriptures I now had to deal, first, with the question of whether I could accept the miracles of Jesus as miracles, and then, whether I could accept the view of his nature which had grown up shortly after the end of his human life: namely that Jesus was not only the son of God (in the sense that we are all sons of God) but also God the Son.

These, too, were issues that Lewis and Griffiths and Merton had dealt with (though I think that for Merton the Incarnation never presented a serious difficulty). For me it was to become a central question, and I wrestled with it for a good long time.

But these questions were not philosophical questions. They were historical questions which led me to examine the witness presented in the Epistles and other writings of the early church. Before I was able to deal effectively with the question of the Incarnation, I came to see that I would have to deal also with the question of interpretation of Scripture, and with the validity and authority of the Christian Church.

So I was soon way over my head in issues which men have wrestled with for centuries and which have profoundly divided Christendom for at least four hundred years. But I could not sidestep these questions. For I came to see that if I was to learn who Jesus was, or at least who I might believe him to be, I would have to come to terms with the fact that all we know of Jesus comes to us on the authority of other human beings; and of their truthfulness and objectivity it is not easy to be certain. Besides which, reasonable and honest men are not able to agree on the meaning of the accounts which these witnesses left to us. So at last I found myself in a thicket of conflicting arguments which required all my resources of thought and discernment to disentangle: a process which brought me towards considerations of doctrine far finer than any I intend to deal with here.

It would not be fair to the reader to pretend that I went about considering these issues in a well-collected, scholarly way. It was a time in my life of great discouragement, even of hopelessness; a time when I had the loneliness of living outside a family circle for the first time; a time of several deep personal disappointments. I wanted the shelter and comfort that religion might provide; and this was itself part of the obstacle. I could not take shelter under a leaky roof. Until I was intellectually convinced that the shelter was sound, religion would be for me no shelter at all. In short, I had something like the difficulty Lewis had, of not being able to accept Christianity because it might be wish fulfillment rather than hard reality. And my longing for religion offered me no psychological comfort. On the contrary, it made me all the lonelier, for I felt different and out of step from most of my contemporaries. They did not seem to share the longing that I felt. They seemed not to need or want anything to do with religion at all, but had dismissed religion out of hand.

At about this time I had an experience which I dare not call mystical, but which affected me very profoundly. I had given up going to church—the Christian Science Church—because it seemed, for me at any rate, both an exercise and a pretense. I was no longer able to accept Christian Science. To sit through a Christian Science service left me bewildered and lost. I wanted to accept it for my family's sake, but could not. Going to church was troubling and unsatisfactory.

On one of these Sunday mornings when I was at home, doing ordinary things like making breakfast and cleaning the apartment, I found myself thinking about God and especially about Jesus Christ. Suddenly the words came into my mind very strongly, almost like a voice, which Jesus had spoken to the disciples when he found them asleep: "Could you not watch with me one hour?"

I know now that in the lives of Christians experiences such as these happen with some frequency. But at the time this prompting seemed to me extraordinary, as though someone or something —I dared not think it was God himself—had spoken to me. This is not to say that I dropped everything at once and began going to church. But I did begin to reflect, for the first time, on the possibility of going to church again, if not in the Christian Science Church, then in some other one. And I knew then, more clearly than before, that it was Jesus Christ I was looking for. He had asked me to watch one hour with him. I began to want to find him and to listen to him: to know what message he wanted to convey.

This moment was, I think, for me, the golden string. And it led me by a very tortuous path, at first. For it was not only intellectual inquiry and study that brought me to where I now am. There were some accidents, some twists of circumstance, that had a part to play. Looking back, one might suppose that these, too, were moments of grace. I do in fact think they were. But on the surface there is nothing remarkable about them. They are, or appear to be, coincidences, nothing more.

After some reflection I decided to attend the Episcopal Church. The choice was based on family feeling. My family had been Episcopalians for generations (until my grandmother and her sisters became Christian Scientists). And I strongly identified with my great-grandmother, Sallie Ball Powell, although I had never known her. She was a much-loved family figure and had been a sincere Episcopalian. There was a need, I think, to find my own spiritual roots and to be in touch with my own family heritage. So the Anglican church was the logical choice. But when I began to attend services, at St. Bartholomew's in Manhattan, it seemed to me more of a social experience than anything else. There was a young people's group, there was a coffee hour after services, but like so many gatherings in New York, it was busy and crowded, and I felt among strangers there as everywhere.

About this time (quite by chance) I met a friend from New Orleans who, like me, had a strong sense of family history. His family and mine had known one another for generations in a tiny Louisiana town called St. Francisville. His ancestors and mine were buried in the same country graveyard.

This friend, whose name was Stone Leake, was a very serious Anglican. He invited me to attend a congregation which he thought very special, the Church of the Resurrection. What attracted him there, I think, was the high liturgy, which was indeed beautifully done. But what I found more attractive was that I felt, for the first time, the fellowship of believing Christians. I felt the presence of faith, though I did not yet understand what I was sensing. However, I was sufficiently at home to want to take instruction there. The spirit in which I did this was not yet one of belief. It was a spirit of inquiry, mingled with doubt. I was not sure that when I understood what Anglicans believed, that I would be able to accept their faith. But I was determined, in any event, to learn more about it.

It now seems to me quite providential that this happened. For the young priest who instructed me, Charles Owen Moore, was a man of good education, sound theology, great sensitivity, and most important of all, I think, of very strong personal faith. I began to go to him for instruction about once a week.

I say it was providential. In fact, I think that without him, or someone very like him, I could never have found my way through the tangle of questions which confronted me. For the issues I was trying to deal with were principally the issues that had been dealt with by the early Church and by the early Councils of the Church: the issues that underlie the Apostle's and the Nicene Creeds. It had not escaped my notice that the Apostle's Creed was fundamental to the Anglican, the Lutheran, and the Roman Catholic faith. In order to become a Christian I would have to be able to say that Creed (at least that one, and possibly several others) with an undivided heart. And that was something I could not yet do. I am told that Queen Victoria, faithful churchwoman that she was, used to cross her fingers at some point in the recitation of the Creed. I was not prepared to follow her example. Either the Christian faith was to be mine—without glossing over the difficult parts—or I could not be a Christian at all.

I do not remember clearly how my dialogue with Father Moore developed at the beginning. But I do remember the first two books he suggested I read. The first, by J. Langmead Casserley, called *No Faith of My Own*, was a clear and simple exposition of the faith once given to the apostles. The second, *Who Moved the Stone?*, had to do with evidence for the Resurrection.

I remember telling Father Moore that I had liked both books. He remarked that while they were favorites of his, they were not helpful to everyone. I began to grasp then how personal the course of an inquiry must be. Each person, groping for faith, finds authors and arguments which correspond to his own cast of mind; and what convinces one person may not convince another.

While I was struggling with the historical questions (and trying to give myself a course in Scriptural exegesis overnight), I came upon the writings of C. S. Lewis. I say I came upon them—but I think it was actually for the second time. Shortly before I had met him, not too happily, in *The Screwtape Letters*, a work which I found both inscrutable and annoying. I could not make head or tail out of the central presumption of that book, namely that of being tempted by external spiritual forces. Was the man actually asking modern people to take angels and devils seriously? It seemed preposterous. In those days I was not ready to understand Christianity as it appears in *The Screwtape Letters:* the practical business of trying to be good. But when I came upon *Mere Christianity*, I had a more rewarding experience. Here was a modern writer advancing reasonable arguments for the existence of God. The most telling of them, I thought, was the argument from conscience as something existing, or coming to exist, almost "spontaneously" in human beings, regardless of their upbringing or conditioning. This notion, that our human sense of the oughtness of things, that things ought to be just and fair, might suggest an ultimate source of justice, God, was an argument which struck me with great force, and I think it was the first good argument I had heard, not for God, but for the kind of God that human beings might be concerned with. In accepting Lewis's argument, that the conscience of Man might be a proof of the justice of God, I also began to perceive conscience as a kind of gift from God: something I had never thought of before.

Shortly thereafter I read both *Miracles* and *The Problem of Pain*. Each one seemed to me to be what I most needed to read at that very moment. Each dealt with a key issue which had been troubling me. I was by now reading the Gospels intently, and I was beginning to see how difficult it would be to subtract the miracles of Jesus from the rest of the account without doing serious damage to the fabric of the story and to the conception of what sort of person Jesus had been. Yet I was not sure I could accept the miracles whole and entire, as I saw other Christians doing. I was profoundly out of sympathy with modern theologians and preachers who tried to explain the miracles away. I was annoyed, for example, at the suggestion that the miracle of the loaves and fishes was an incident in which those present really had enough food with them but refused to share it until Jesus's preaching changed their hearts. I simply could not accept interpretations of that kind, which seemed complete contradictions of the Gospel records. At the same time, I had difficulty twisting my reason around to accept the miracles. Lewis began to make for me a real bridge there between reason and faith.

In *The Problem of Pain* he dealt with a still more troubling question. How can God, if he is good, permit us to suffer? And he met it head on, no shilly-shallying. In the process, he expounded the ancient Christian doctrines on free will and sin and good and evil in a way that seemed to me fresh and new. He even managed to make me think—at least for the moment—that both heaven and hell were real.

By this time I was beginning to see that there were in modern times a number of people of sharp perceptions and keen wit who actually did believe Christianity, not in any softened, modernized version, but in all the roughness and strangeness of its ancient form. I realized, too, that while the Gospel accounts were not history in the usual sense, they had a firmer historical validity than I had been led to believe. Like Griffiths (I was to learn later), I began to be persuaded by the way the Gospels "sounded." They seemed to me less like a Greek myth and more like an account of events which had actually taken place. But it was not only the Gospels which affected me in this way. If anything, I was even more persuaded by the Acts of the Apostles and the Epistles. The seemingly bizarre events which they recorded seemed to me as unlike a made-up story as anything could be.

About this time I came across the J. B. Phillips translation of the letters of Paul, called *Letters to Young Churches*. Attached as I was to the King James Version, I had never read any other translation of the Bible. I found somehow that this modern translation struck me as the King James Version had not done. As a student of Latin I knew what it was to read something in the original, how much stronger and clearer the author's thought was in his own words, rather than in the translator's. But I had also come to appreciate the value of a good idiomatic translation. Phillips's rendering of the letters made me wish I could read them in Greek and made me feel, at the same time, that I was doing so. In this translation I came somehow closer to the thought of Paul. He was no longer a distant, legendary figure but a very immediate, human one.

And Paul had lived at the same time as others who had known Jesus. He knew men and women who actually had witnessed the events of the Crucifixion and who insisted upon the fact of the Resurrection. Skeptics were fond of pointing out that the Gospels had been written later on, perhaps with interweaving myths and exaggerations. But this was not true of Paul's letters. I began to feel that these letters were either a true account or the most extraordinary fabrication ever concocted.

I knew, of course, that the writers of the Epistles might have been somehow misguided. But as I continued my reading, I became less and less able to convince myself of this. An important contribution to my thought at this stage came from Lewis and Bede Griffiths, for they seemed able to trust New Testament documents—at least as much as other first-century documents: Livy and Sallust and Tacitus. And they did not believe that the observations of the ancients were any less reliable than those of modern people.

By this time I was reading straight through the New Testament and it was affecting me deeply. I could not get over the conviction that Jesus was real. In reading the Arthurian legend or the stories of Homer, I had felt that a historical figure was being made larger by the inventive powers of the story teller. In the New Testament my impression was just the opposite. It seemed to me that the Gospel writers were not able to capture the largeness of the figure about whom they were writing. There seemed, too, to be parts of the story which were very odd, which did not fit—in the sense of a smooth literary whole—with other parts of the story. Curious things were included, such as the reluctance of Jesus to heal Gentiles, his insistence upon secrecy in certain of his healings, his use of spit to anoint the eyes of the blind man, the detail—at the raising of Lazarus—of the sisters' insistence that their brother's body was already giving off a stench of decay. These sometimes unpleasant details seemed to lend greater credibility to the story. And yet, the more I read it, the more incredible was the tale.

I found a parallel to the experience I was having when I came to read Griffiths' *The Golden String.* He, too, had experienced a sense of truthfulness and authenticity in his reading of the Gospels. And he had experienced something else which I recognized. He had found the account of Jesus in the New Testament "far different from what I had been led to suppose." What surprised him was that the miraculous events and the human elements in the life of Jesus were woven together in such a way that it would be almost impossible to suppose them of different sources or origins. Everything was told with the same quality and seemed to belong to the whole. "The human teaching which I had always loved," he writes, "was implicated . . . with supernatural claims of an astonishing kind, which had the same quality of authentic utterance." So for Griffiths, as for me, the persuasiveness of the Gospels themselves became an issue in the Dialectic. I think that for me this was the first real stirring of faith. But I also experienced this difficulty: If one were to accept Jesus Christ, it would be necessary to accept him as the Gospels portrayed him. One could not take the human Jesus and leave the supernatural Jesus alone.

Up to this point I had been willing to think of Jesus as a godly man, even a godlike man. I could think of him as Master; I could even call him Lord, according to a definition of my own. But what I found enormously difficult to believe was that Jesus was

God. I remembered a conversation I had had with a Catholic cousin of mine when we were both young children, perhaps seven or eight. He had insisted to me that Jesus was God, and I had been profoundly shocked. I had maintained that Jesus was the son of God, but not God the Son. (Lewis is right in saying that our most important thinking is done before the age of fourteen.) My cousin's assertion had seemed to me shocking—blasphemous, if I had known the word—for I knew there was only one God (the Father) and did not see how Jesus could be God without violating the concept of God as one. Even as an adult I was troubled by any notion of a man as God. It felt pagan to me, almost barbaric.

Up to this point I had felt sure that this title had never been claimed by Jesus himself. I had assumed that this title had been thrust upon him by the superstitious piety of those who lived after him. Though I must have known certain texts which can be quoted in behalf of the divinity of Christ, I had interpreted them figuratively. I am thinking in particular of the statement, "I and my Father are one." I had always taken this to mean that Jesus was in harmony with the Father's will. Now I was beginning, as I read the New Testament straight through, to find that there are many such texts, not the least of which is, "Before Abraham was, I am." It was possible to interpret some of them as I had been doing; but to interpret all of them in this way—that is, to find alternative interpretations for what Jesus meant in each instance—was more complex and required more cerebration than to accept on its face value the astonishing claim that Jesus had made. He had claimed not only to be God's chosen one, but also to be acting with the authority of God himself. Indeed, he had all but said, "I am God."

This realization—which came to me from reading the Scriptures "for myself"—quite unnerved me. Up to that time I had believed that the title of God the Son had been assigned to Jesus by his devout followers generations, even centuries after his death; that a holy and devout religious leader (like Buddha) had been elevated to deity by the piety and superstition of ancient peoples. Now I could no longer believe this. It began to seem to me that there were only two possible interpretations: either he was who he claimed to be, or he was a madman. The other interpretations which I had been cherishing—that Jesus was the holiest of men, a great spiritual master, greater perhaps than any other, but in the mode, somehow, of Moses and Buddha and the Prophets—seemed now to be ruled out. I was left with only two choices. And both of them seemed to me rather extreme.

I had now passed quite irrevocably beyond Mrs. Eddy's statement (with which I had grown up) that "Jesus of Nazareth was the most scientific man that ever trod the globe."[19] By scientific, I think Mrs. Eddy meant spiritually insightful. I now found it possible to believe him that, but that one must either believe him more than that or reject him entirely. No other options seemed plausible, in the context of the New Testament itself. And I could not imagine any authority or corroboration which could help me to accept this extraordinary belief—that is, any authority except that of God himself.

It may appear from this brief account of my progress through the New Testament that I have glossed over some of the difficulties and problems presented by New Testament scholarship. Nothing could be further from the truth—at least as far as my own intellectual course was concerned. I was aware then, as I am now, of the many controversies which exist with regard to the Gospel texts, dating of various passages, questions relating to authorship and interpolation, and the possibility of some pious legends having crept in. At the same time I began to see how much any knowledge of Jesus rests, humanly, upon the testimony of human beings and is mediated through their historical situations and personal limitations. I began to see that I would never have through scholarship and study any more hard evidence than I already had in hand. When I came to this fork in the road, I felt that I had come as far as reason and logic could take me. I was beginning to understand for the first time what is meant by an act of faith: a leap, not without trust, not without a framework of reason and thought, but a risk-taking jump into a realm beyond logic and reason.

I began to envy those who had known Jesus and could judge his credibility at firsthand. I began to envy those who had known those who had known Jesus. How could I evaluate the credibility of people whom I had never known? At the same time my mind began to dwell on the incident in which the Risen Jesus shows himself to doubting Thomas, and Thomas comes to believe in the Resurrection. I felt like a blow the force of the words, "Blessed are those who have not seen and yet have believed."

About this time I must have discovered the writings of Ronald Knox, for I remember reading that Knox, too, had wrestled with the problem of Jesus as either lunatic or divine. Knox wrote brilliantly of the instances throughout the Gospels which seem to convict Jesus of paranoia: the insistence upon secrecy, the intimation to his closest friends that he is the one person to save the world, the hints of a great trial to come. What might seem to theologians like foreknowledge of the Crucifixion could also be interpreted as the ravings of a madman, one who might seek his own death in order to demonstrate his greatness. Certainly the world has produced a number of them! I thought of the assassins of great men who attack the established order to fulfill their own need for greatness. Knox, too, seemed to think there was plausibility in this interpretation. But he had worked out a scheme whereby the same events were exactly what would have occurred in the event that the Incarnation had actually taken place. I was not sure I could believe as firmly as he did. But I also felt sure that the disciples could have recognized madness as easily as anyone!

It was clear to me now that argument and study could not resolve this question. There was simply not enough evidence in hand. I speculated on what modern psychologists would have thought of Jesus, had they subjected him to examinations. It occurred to me that even if Jesus were the Son of God, he might have looked like a lunatic under the light of scientific inquiry. Science was little help, not so much because of the lack of real information, but because the nature of the question was beyond science. It had to be dealt with in a different realm, with a very different kind of conceptual thinking.

Perhaps I have given the impression that my course of reading and reflection came about in a logical, linear way. It may also seem that I only read books by believing Christians. In fact, the course of my thought was very much a zigzag. Often, when I felt myself becoming convinced or persuaded by believers, I ran from that and deliberately plunged myself into the opposite point of view. I knew the emotional power which Christianity had for me, but I did not want to be overcome by that. So, from time to time, perhaps not consciously, I administered an antidote. When I went to the writings of atheists, it was not only for the sake of being fair-minded; the fact was that I did not know from which direction clarity and resolution of my difficult questions would come.

I have already mentioned Julian Huxley's *Religion Without Revelation*. In Ashley Montagu's *Immortality*, I found a good case made for Christian teaching as an aspect of wish fulfillment. In the writings of Robert Graves, I did not find (at least in the books I read) any organized attack on religious belief, yet his treatment of Christian myths together with those of pagan cultures (which I now think a very suitable and appropriate thing to do) then seemed to call into doubt the validity of what Christians, and especially Catholics, believed and believe. Graves did not seem to me to be "out to get" religion; indeed, he had a deep respect and understanding for myth and poetry as religious—a fundamental encounter with mystery—which was profoundly appealing; yet the effect of his scholarly and sensitive assembling of mythical elements from many sources had the effect on me then of making the Christian story seem less true: a "made-up story" which had somehow been added on to the historical facts of Jesus' life.

I found myself able to wrestle with Huxley and Montagu and Russell—perhaps because their attitudes were so argumentative. Their positions were stated in debating-society terms and I tended to respond in kind. Russell, for example, though renowned as a philosopher, seemed to be using a very shallow style of argumentation. He argued for example that Jesus was not wise (because the Second Coming did not occur promptly) nor kind (because Jesus preached about hell and awakened terror in the hearts of men). He argued against Christian morality by mentioning promi-

nent Christians who did not practice it; he delivered his most telling argument—that religion is based on fear of the unknown and
a desire for protection—simply as an assertion, to be accepted at
face value. Oddly enough, while I could not fault his logic, I
found his argument unpersuasive. Perhaps it was because his viewpoint seemed to lack depth and humanity. He professed not to
understand why people seemed to feel a need for some sense of
order and purpose in the universe; he seemed to think that by
stamping out tiresome religious notions he was doing humanity a
service. Perhaps I did not share his optimistic view that—with
God safely out of the universe—man could proceed to conquer
the future by the force of his own intelligence and courage.

But where Graves was concerned, the going was more difficult.
Graves did not seem to be making an argument. Indeed, he was
writing not about religion but about poetry and myth. He was
able to show the mythological character of much of Christian tradition and belief; but he did not do so as though he were trying to
discredit Christianity. This way of approaching the question was
far more unsettling to me than the arguments of Russell and
Montagu and Huxley. In fact, he did not seem to feel the need to
state that religious belief was primitive and obsolete. To him, it
appeared to be self-evident. In *The White Goddess*, Graves says
of Sir James Frazer that what he was implicitly saying was that
"Christian legend, dogma and ritual are the refinement of a great
body of primitive and even barbarous beliefs, and that almost the
only original element in Christianity is the personality of Jesus."[20]
This appeared to be Graves's position too. It was in fact a commonplace viewpoint, the one most popular among the people I
had known in college, at any rate those who bothered to reflect on
the question at all. And there were moments when I found it very
plausible. (Sometimes I still do.)

But in the end, I think, I was able to identify with Lewis's resolution of the matter: Could not Christianity be a true myth, the
one towards which all the others were leading, and for which they
were a foretaste and a preparation?

I do not, in fact, think that my resolution of this matter was an
intellectual one at all. I did not find that Lewis's argument was

more reasonable or more authentic or more plausible than that of Frazer and Graves. Instead I think I *identified* with Lewis because I had had the same experience of mythology and legend which he had. I had experienced God not only in the Christian myths but in the pagan ones; and I was beginning to trust, because of his experience, something that I had not until then trusted in my own experience: human powers of invention and imagination, not as forms of self-deception, but as ways to truth.

With regard to Huxley and Montagu, where they touched on immortality the story is somewhat different. As yet, I found this aspect of Christian teaching the least persuasive of all. I knew it was the dream towards which the poets had been reaching from the earliest times. But I could not conceive of its being true. I think I did not find the idea of heaven attractive or consoling. I do not think I even accepted any notion of heaven; instead I thought of the issue as a matter of life after death. Even if there were such a life, that did not cancel out the necessity of dying, losing this consciousness of things; the notion of living on, somehow, afterwards, was not consoling or even plausible to me. I think Huxley and Montagu got to me on this point because my mindset was like theirs to begin with; perhaps, like Lewis, I did not want immortality. My notions of immortality were influenced by the classical writers I had read. I remembered the myth of Tithonus who was given immortality, without being given eternal youth to go along with it; Greek and Roman deities were fond of having little practical jokes like that. So, where immortality was concerned, I thought the skeptics had the better of the argument. But somehow, arguments against immortality did not strike at the heart of the question. Immortality then seemed to me a somewhat ancillary matter. To argue against immortality was not to argue against all of belief, I thought, but only one part of Christian doctrine.

I had come now to a point where the use of the intellect was no longer helpful. Arguments had brought me far, but not far enough. I sensed that every position had its weaknesses; neither the atheist nor the believer could present an open-and-shut case. Reason, I began to think, was an imperfect tool. In the Shapley film, I had come to see how limited man's knowledge of the universe must ultimately be; there were definite terms on the things he could see and hear and learn; now I saw that his reasoning powers also had limits. Some things could never be attained by reason.

So it became plain that both atheism and belief, as Mortimer Adler has put it, are faith positions. Each is a definite choice of a construct of existence that leaps beyond reason. And agnosticism is the refusal to make any leap at all. But how was I to choose? Was I to spend the rest of my life in a game of intellectual shuttlecock, driven back and forth between one position and the other? Or should I agnostically throw up my hands and admit that the whole thing was undecipherable? In some part of myself, I thought that, too, would be a choice.

I had come to a crossing and I did not know how I could get across. Up to now, I had been encouraged to find that people of reason could be believers. But I now saw that they do so with a power in themselves which is beyond the rational. They exert a faculty which Phillips calls (I have since learned) the faculty of faith. But it is possible (until one has exerted this power for himself) to regard its use as an exercise in self-delusion.

It was the will which now had to be brought into play (and some modern thinkers did not even believe in the will itself). A choice had to be made. And though I saw the issue clearly, I did not yet have the courage, the heart, the conviction to make the choice which lay before me. I had come to the end of that part of the journey which I now call the Dialectic. And I felt that something else remained, that there was still a distance to go. A new part of the experience was beginning. In fact, it had already begun.

4

Struggle

What follows the Dialectic is a period I call Struggle. I cannot say
with any certainty how it begins, how the convert moves from one
phase to another. It seems the only proper explanation would be
that it comes from following one's nose or the yellow brick road.
Of this movement one might as easily write, "And then Dorothy
and her friends found themselves in a different part of the woods,
where the undergrowth was more tangled than before." Somehow
or other (I must apologize for the vagueness of this language) it
seems that a tiny seed of faith has taken root, is beginning to
struggle for existence, but does not yet have the vigor to sprout
and grow. In the Dialectic, the convert was weighing two possi-
bilities of equal value, vacillating between them; now he has made
a movement, however slight, in the direction of faith. What takes
him across this border? Even converts themselves, knowing this
passage as intimately as anyone, cannot fully account for what has
taken place.

Something which—for lack of a better name—we must call the
will has taken over and moved the spirit into a realm where intellect cannot go. This "will" seems almost instinctive. It springs not
from thought but from some other part of the consciousness. Yet

it is more than instinct. It is a choosing, an action deliberately taken. Whether through reason or insight or imagination, the spirit has glimpsed some other kind of possible life which is different from the life lived up to now. To have that life, the convert must choose it, must reach out for it with both hands.

In trying to describe this unique action I am reminded of the problems posed by early Greek philosophers who tried to deal by reason with the observable facts of motion. It seemed to them logical that, in order to cross a given distance, the mover must go half the distance each time, then half the remaining distance, and again, half, ad infinitum. In this manner it would never be possible, these philosophers reasoned, to cross from one side of the street to the other. For however often half the distance was crossed, there would still be a half, however infinitely small, remaining. Crossing the street was a logical impossibility. But the fact was that, after a number of such halfway crossings, the boot of the mover would be touching the opposite curbstone. So, too, with the movement from reason to faith, the problem is solved by action, not by thought.

Solvitur ambulando, said the ancient philosophers; in our case, the answer is *solvitur credendo.* I do not offer this as an explanation for the crossing from Dialectic to Struggle. I simply say that it does take place, and converts themselves cannot always say why or how.

What seems to have happened in my own case was that once my reason had established the authenticity of two equal and opposite positions (atheism and belief), I came to a point where one was more plausible to me than another. I did so after a time (I don't know how long) of lingering in indecision; but that time simply ended. I knew that the time for hesitation was past.

Even as I made my first hesitant choice, however, I felt that what I was entering upon was not a sure thing but a gamble. I began to see the issue as a conflict between two warring parties in the universe and within me. And those parties seemed to be the forces of life and light arrayed against the forces of darkness and death. I am not now speaking of immortality—for that question was one I had hardly yet considered. I am speaking instead of how

the issue seemed to me, how the choice looked as it lay before me.
It seemed to me that I had to choose either something which was
hard, but life-giving, or something else, less difficult, easy in fact,
but which had about it a kind of hopelessness and despair. But
there were no clear guidelines; some guessing was involved; it was
a gamble in which one must cast one's lot with one side or the
other, with the believers or the skeptics. And in casting this lot, I
could not be fully sure what cause I was joining, or whether it
might not even be a lost cause. Certainly it seemed to me at that
moment to be an unpopular cause. I wondered if the ranks were a
bit thin, made up of poorly trained recruits, old women, children,
the emotionally wounded, the halt and the blind.

In the stories of Chesterton and Lewis which I read later, I
came upon this particular vision of mine expressed in fictional
terms: the whole universe was at war, and one must line up with
God's agents or his opponents. What a simplistic notion! A projection, psychologists would no doubt say, of the conflict between
good and evil which we feel within ourselves. But when I met the
idea in Lewis and Chesterton it was with a spark of recognition,
of identification. It was a notion I had met before—was it in Milton's *Paradise Lost*? Was it in Spenser? Was it in the Bible? No, I
had met it long before that. . . . I had met it within myself.

It began to seem to me, in short, that whether one conceived of
goodness as something in the universe outside us, or in the world
within us, it was not only real but alive, but that in order to have
it, one must choose it, and that to choose it would be to choose
life, however appearances might argue to the contrary.

It may seem that I am getting ahead of my story. But I am
not yet speaking of Surrender. I am speaking of[the first movement, a mere leaning or tilting, a first casting off from shore. It is
after this first tentative choice that one begins to find oneself in a
sea of bewilderment, assayed by doubts and difficulties]of every
sort; and these sometimes quite beyond the powers of the intellect
to set aside.

[This struggle is the crisis of conversion: the most difficult time
of all. It requires of us a kind of introspection and self-reflection
which we have not done before. It is, if not the first, then the

deepest encounter with the self which we have made, a confrontation with our own weakness and failures and inadequacies which is, to say the very least, disconcerting. This conflict is both a struggle against belief and a struggle against the self; and it is accompanied with a sense of uneasiness, of being cut loose from one's familiar emotional moorings,] not knowing when, if ever, one will touch land again.

This is not to say that the use of reason has been altogether left behind; only that reason is no longer the method by which any progress can be made; by this time the doubts and questions which remain are beyond reason. Some other mode of progress is needed, and it seems as though it will have to be invented, learned by experience for the first time: our customary ways of dealing with reality seem to be of no help at all.

To understand this part of the conversion process, I think we must begin to look at it from the viewpoint of faith. To skeptics, the conflicts of the struggle may seem merely to be neurotic, the resolution of conflicts within the personality. To believers, however, the same events appear otherwise.

To pursue for a moment this sense of a war or conflict between Good and Evil. Surely this is one of the fundamental tensions of human experience. Looking at it from the perspective of science, or skepticism, it is possible to say that it is a merely psychological phenomenon. It is an aspect of the development of conscience; it is conceived of in a childlike way; it is the stuff of the Unconscious, presented to us in a myth or story; one might almost call it a formula, so many great stories have been founded on it; and yet when we encounter it anew in fiction—the universe of Tolkien might be one example—we meet it with a spark of recognition. Mythical or not, there is something here which strikes us as real, as true. We have experienced this conflict within ourselves. Believers think that this goodness and evil within ourselves is a reflection of the way things really are, not only within ourselves, but in every reality. To say that they are psychological—which they are—is not to say that they are therefore less real or less true.

For Lewis and some of his contemporaries, one of the great barriers to be crossed was that of "chronological snobbery"—the idea that what the ancients had believed was somehow, by the very passage of time and the development of thought, out of date. I had had the same difficulty and had dealt with it. But a greater difficulty which now confronted me was the argument from psychology. For me, and for my generation, the term "psychological" had become what the term "medieval" was for others: a way of dismissing a phenomenon as a quirk, an aberration, an appearance rather than a reality.

So in the Struggle I had to contend with the realization that religious experience was in part psychological, and to determine whether I must therefore dismiss it as "only psychological." This was perhaps my greatest difficulty. I could see clearly that I had emotional needs in my own life, dispositions which were very likely the result of my own childhood and adolescence. I had not had a close adolescent relationship with my father. I wondered if I was turning to God the Father as a substitute. In my college years, I had been very close to my mother and grandmother, perhaps more dependent than other people of my age on family ties. I wondered if my movement towards religion was a late outcropping of adolescent rebelliousness, the need to establish an independent identity of my own. Looking back, I see that it may have been related to both of these things. But I now see that if it was, it was not therefore an invalid movement. Then, however, I was inclined to think that if I could identify any psychological need as an underpinning for my movement towards faith, then faith itself was a mere invention of my own to satisfy that need. I feared that I was inventing God because I needed his protection and care. It seemed to me that others I knew did not have the same need for God that I had. So I saw my own need for religion as a sign of some infirmity and was tempted to think that religion itself might be a crutch for the emotionally infirm.

It is hard to say whether difficulties of this sort are dealt with, ultimately, by the reason or by the emotions. But in my own case they seemed to resolve themselves by the passage of time, the experience of maturation, and the practice of faith. Over time, as I began to practice the faith and live as a Christian, I realized that

Christianity does not solve one's emotional problems. And I realized that the emotional problems of Christians do not invalidate Christianity. There are emotionally unsure and emotionally healthy persons on both sides of the issue; and no one contends that the emotional condition of atheists invalidates atheism. It can be argued, for example, that atheists are atheists because of their childhood formation; that they resist God because they hated their fathers and hate all authority. I would not argue in this way. I prefer to think that atheists have made a choice as honest as my own. I think it is a wrong choice. But I respect their position as a reasoned and intellectually honest one.

I came at last to see that the difficulties I have just mentioned—of thinking that God could not possibly be real because he was so much the "answer" to my emotional needs—were barriers that I myself was making against God in my own life. I was dwelling on myself. I was concentrating on my own limitations. I was saying, in some way I didn't fully understand then, that God couldn't possibly exist because I had invented him. Also, I think I thought he was a good deal more than I deserved. (This, of course, was very true. However, it is also true of every other human being!) So in yielding to this line of thought—that God could not exist because he was too good to be true—I was setting myself up as the judge of what ought to be true and what kind of justice ought to prevail in the universe! And all in the guise of reasonable thought, objectivity, and honest self-evaluation!

How did I get beyond this self-centered mentality? Surely, not by any effort of my own. I cannot think that in my state of mind I was able to be any better or less self-centered than I was. Now I have to fall back on that familiar phrase—"by the grace of God." For what power could have entered into my life and brought me up out of what Bunyan calls "the slough of despond" —what power other than goodness itself? I did not deserve God's intervention at that point, that is quite clear. But because his standards are rather different from my own, he gave it to me anyway.

Looking back on this particular turning, I have cause to say, "There but for the grace of God go I." How long might I have continued in this state of entirely selfish personal misery? Nowadays, the term "grace" is somewhat unfashionable in theology—I note that current writers try to express this concept in other, perhaps less old-fashioned language. But converts experience this power in their own lives—a power, not an overwhelming one, but a gentle yet definite leading which takes them out of themselves, gives them the strength to look away from their own inward conflicts and outward towards others, and to God himself.

It is in this way that we come to think that faith is not earned but given; to speak of God's favor; to sense that he has made us through his power something that we could never have made of ourselves on our own.

So in the phase which I call Struggle, I came to see for the first time—by direct experience—that conversion is not something we do ourselves but which God does in us. I could make myself knowledgeable. But my knowledge could not "solve the problem." I could try to be open to reality. But that openness sometimes caused me pain—when I saw how inadequate, how limited, how weak I was. When I try to say how it was I finally became a Christian, I can say only, "It was a gift, and one which I probably did not deserve."

Let me give another example of one of the difficulties I had at this time—a difficulty which I myself was powerless to resolve—the question of the meaning of the Eucharist. I think it shows clearly how little any human exertion or intellectual inquiry can bring us to faith. Christians assemble for a prayer service, bringing bread and wine. Their minister repeats the words that Jesus spoke at the Last Supper. The bread and wine appear as they did before, but Christians believe that in this ceremony something real and fundamental is happening. Now the bread and wine are no longer what they were, but the Lord is really present. The bread and wine, in some mysterious way, are his body and blood. In memory of him they consume them, believing not only in his presence but in the transforming power of the Eucharist itself. But to attend a Eucharistic service without faith is to be unable to see this. The bread and wine appear no different in any material way than they did before. Yet Christians believe some extraordinary thing is taking place. And they believe not only that impossibility, but also that this repeated action draws together and joins all who receive it through the power of God's love. How was I to come to believe that, when I had not believed it before? What power on earth could bring me to it?

Again, I cannot say for certain how this difficulty was for me eventually put to rest. But I do think that I must not discount what Christians call witness: the faith of believers themselves, which shines forth in their lives and from their hearts and influences others profoundly. When I first began to attend Eucharistic services at this time in my own Struggle, I did not understand them, nor did I believe in what was happening. But I could see that others did believe it. And, more than that, I could see that their belief and their love were moving them, were transforming them. I could not see the reality of the Eucharist in the bread and wine, but I could see it in the people who received it. And this, too, I think, was a kind of special grace for me.

Why is it that at this critical time we meet certain others who influence us and lead us, almost by their very existence? I cannot say. But the fact is that I did, and others do. And this witness can be as formidable as the witness of the saints who went to the Colosseum and the furnace for their faith; the witness of (in my case) dozens of seminarians and priests swarming about the corner of Madison Avenue and Fiftieth Street and causing me to wonder, "What do they know that I don't know?"; the witness of simple acts of charity performed by believers towards one another, and to others who do not believe. It is the witness of those who proclaim their faith in books (Lewis, and Griffiths, and Chesterton, and Sayers) with a flinty intellectual precision which makes us say, "They believe it, why can't I?" It is the witness, sometimes, of conversions taking place before our very eyes. When our friends "go over," as the expression has it, we feel that they have abandoned us in our struggle; but at the same time we want to follow them.

Lewis describes this moment in his life—the witness of the conversion of his friends—as something which profoundly unnerved him:

It was then that a really dreadful thing (dreadful to me) happened. First Harwood (still without changing his expression) and then Barfield, embraced the doctrines of Steiner and became Anthroposophists. I was hideously shocked. Everything that I had labored so hard to expel from my own life seemed to have flared up and met me in my best friends.[1]

To be sure, Harwood and Barfield were not accepting Christianity; but that they would accept any supernatural viewpoint at all seemed to Lewis like a betrayal. With his characteristic "chronological snobbery," Lewis objected to their behavior as "medieval." Next Lewis, in a discussion class at Oxford, met and made friends with a "man after my own heart" whose name was Nevill Coghill. He was soon shocked to learn that Coghill, whom he thought the most intelligent and best-informed man in the class—was a Christian and a supernaturalist. And there were other qualities in Coghill which Lewis admired but which seemed to him archaic. Lewis lists these as chivalry, honor, courtesy, "freedom" and "gentilesse."

Lewis admired Coghill as he admired Chesterton, in spite of his Christianity. But now he began to feel surrounded, both by his friends and by the writers he most admired. The books, he says, were beginning to turn against him, for he began to see all at once how every writer with whom he felt a kinship was a Christian. George MacDonald had affected him more than any other writer, but Lewis had admired him in spite of his Christianity. Chesterton had moved him more than all the other moderns, except for his Christianity. He fully trusted Johnson, but found the same quirk in him. Oddly enough, Spenser and Milton had the same turn of mind. Of the ancient authors the most religious were the ones who meant most to him: Plato, Aeschylus, Virgil. The writers with whom he ought to have sympathized—Shaw, Wells, Mill, Gibbon and Voltaire—"all seemed a little thin," Lewis remarks.

The more he read, the more this preference became plain to Lewis. There was *The Dream of the Rood*; he was moved "more deeply still" by Langland; "intoxicated" by John Donne; "satisfied" by Thomas Browne. George Herbert was "alarming" because he so succeeded in conveying "the very quality of life as we actually live it from moment to moment"; but Herbert had the same quirk. "The wretched fellow," Lewis complains, "instead of doing it all directly, insisted on mediating it through what I would still have called 'the Christian mythology.' "[2] At the same time the writers Lewis was reading (who might be thought the precoursors of modern enlightenment) did not touch him. Bacon bored him, he did not care for Restoration comedy, and thought Byron's *Don Juan* tiresome. The only non-Christians who made any appeal to him were the Romantics, and they, too, were "dangerously tinged with something like religion, even at times with Christianity." At the same time Lewis resisted the obvious conclusion—that there might be something to this belief that his favorite writers cherished. He concluded instead that the idealism to which Christians assented (through this outmoded and unbelievable mythology of theirs) made them better and more attractive because it caused them to strive for a high standard; nothing more.

But the conspiracy against Lewis continued. In his real-life associations he continued to make friends with Christians. He mentions in particular H. V. D. Dyson and J. R. R. Tolkien. Of Tolkien he says, "Friendship (with him) marked the breakdown of two old prejudices. At my first coming into the world, I had been (implicitly) warned never to trust a Papist and, at my first coming into the English faculty (explicitly), never to trust a philologist. Tolkien was both."[3]

It was in fact both Dyson and Tolkien who assisted Lewis towards his acceptance of Christ, and they did so in a memorable evening of conversation which took place on September 19, 1931. Lewis had just read A *Winter's Tale* and had seen in it a myth of the Resurrection. It was in this mood that he entertained Dyson and Tolkien in his rooms at Magdalen. Walter Hooper and Roger Lancelyn Green have described the event quite well in their biography of Lewis. They describe how the three friends strolled up Addison's walk, discussing myth and metaphor, until a windstorm drove them into Lewis's rooms, where they talked until three in the morning. Then Tolkien left to go home; Lewis and Dyson saw him through the little postern door that opens onto Magdalen Bridge, and continued talking for another hour.

One is tempted to think that Oxford is holy ground; for the walk that Tolkien and Dyson and Lewis took is reminiscent of the walk taken by Newman through Christ Church Meadow with the Reverend William James, then Fellow of Oriel, one that was to have a decisive influence on Newman's Christianity. And the walk that those three men took—two men of faith striving to share that faith with another—reminds us how humanly conversion takes place, on certain evenings in particular places and bounded by human limitations. Through such human contacts the grace of God seems to move from one life to another.

Several days later (October 1) Lewis wrote to his boyhood friend Arthur Greeves (a Christian): "I have just passed on from believing in God to definitely believing in Christ—in Christianity."[4]

"What I couldn't see," Lewis explained to Greeves, in a letter some days later, "was how the life and death of Someone Else (whoever he was) 2,000 years ago could help us here and now—except in so far as his *example* helped us. And the example business, though true and important, is not Christianity: right in the centre of Christianity, in the Gospels and St. Paul, you keep on getting something quite different and mysterious, expressed in those phrases I have so often ridiculed ('propitiation'—'sacrifice'—'the blood of the Lamb') expressions which I could only interpret in senses that seemed to me either silly or shocking.

"Now what Dyson and Tolkien showed me was this: that if I met the idea of a sacrifice in a pagan story, I didn't mind it at all: again, that if I met the idea of a god sacrificing himself to himself . . . I liked it very much and was mysteriously moved by it: again, that the idea of the dying and reviving God (Balder, Adonis, Bacchus) similarly moved me provided I met it anywhere *except* in the Gospels. The reason was that in the Pagan stories I was prepared to feel the myth as profound and suggestive of meanings beyond my grasp even though I could not say in cold prose 'what it meant.' Now the story of Christ is simply a true myth: a myth working on us in the same way as others, but with this tremendous difference that it really happened; and one must be content to accept it in the same way, remembering that it is God's myth where the others are men's myths. . . ."[5]

And Dyson and Tolkien were not the only ones who influenced Lewis towards his acceptance of Christ. Another influence came from a totally unexpected source: a person whom Lewis called the "hardest-boiled atheist" he knew. This unidentified guest of his observed that the evidence for the historicity of the Gospels was excellent: "Rum thing. All that stuff of Frazer's about the Dying God. Rum thing. It almost looks as if it had really happened once."

Although this episode took place years before Lewis's walk with Dyson and Tolkien in Oxford, and might be thought of as part of his dialectic rather than part of the final phase of his conversion, I think it is part of the phenomenon which seems to occur to many converts in their final wrestling with the Lord: the sense of being surrounded. Lewis says that at the end, God, through his believing friends and acquaintances, and even through the opinions of nonbelievers, was beginning to "close in" on him. "If even a hard-boiled atheist, the cynic of cynics, the toughest of the toughs, was not, as I would still have put it—'safe'—where could I turn? Was there then no escape?"[6]

In a letter to still another friend, Lewis observed that he was becoming (very gradually and reluctantly) drawn towards Christian belief. And he shows that he now sees himself not as the seeker but as the sought: ". . . whereas once I would have said, 'Shall I adopt Christianity?' I am now waiting to see whether it will adopt me: i.e. I know that there is another Party in the affair, —that I'm playing Poker, not Patience, as I once supposed."[7]

Lewis was feeling the pressure of the chase, the tension of a great gamble in which the stakes were nothing other than his own life. And he was definitely on the run.

In *Surprised by Joy*, he says: "The fox had been dislodged from the Hegelian wood and was now running in the open . . . bedraggled and weary, hounds barely a field behind. And nearly everyone was now (one way or another) in the pack: Plato, Dante, Macdonald, Herbert, Barfield, Tolkien, Dyson, Joy itself. Everyone and everything had joined the other side. Even my own pupil Griffiths—now Dom Bede Griffiths—did his share."[8]

I am not suggesting, precisely, that there was anything other-worldly about the way in which Lewis was surrounded. (Strictly speaking, is there anything so remarkable about the conversion to Christianity of a man whose closest friends were Christians and who spent a good deal of his time reading Christian authors?) Yet I cannot fail to observe that something very similar happened to Merton too. Not all of Merton's close friends at Columbia (he had a definite circle of them) were Christians. Yet it seems, at the end, that they all conspired to make him one. What unnerved Merton was that they seemed able to perceive Christianity at a deeper level than he did, even though many of them did not fully accept Christianity themselves. Of this period in his life Merton says:

> So now it is time to tell a thing that I could not realize then, but which has become very clear to me: that God brought me and a half dozen others together at Columbia, and made us friends, in such a way that our friendship would work powerfully to rescue us from the confusion and misery in which we had come to find ourselves. . . .[9]

There was Mark Van Doren, one of Merton's professors, whose way of teaching poetry opened Merton's mind to a realm it had not glimpsed before: "Mark's balanced and sensitive clear way of seeing things . . . being fundamentally scholastic, though not nec-essarily and explicitly Christian, presented [the most important realities] in ways that made them live within us. . . ."

Of another friend, Bob Lax, Merton says that he had "a kind of natural, instinctive spirituality, a kind of inborn direction to the living God. . . ." with a mind naturally disposed "to a kind of affinity for Job and St. John of the Cross."[10]

Then there was Bob Gibney, who was interested in scholastic philosophy "in much the way James Joyce was," Merton says. He respected it, but his respect was intellectual. There was not enough genuine attraction in it to bring about a conversion. Gibney, Merton says, was waiting for a sign: "some kind of a sensible and tangible interior jolt from God, to get him started."[11] Gibney kept waiting. His life did not dispose him towards the action of grace. With the exception of Ed Rice, who was a Catholic, none of Merton's friends at Columbia were Christian believers at this time. Yet the effect of their friendship was to bring him to religion.

At the same time Merton was being led towards Christianity by his reading. He was doing a graduate paper on Blake, and Blake's Christianity was affecting him deeply. But at the same time he was moved by authors not yet (or never to be) Christians. Aldous Huxley's book, *Ends and Means,* showed Huxley accepting mystical experience. This seems to have affected Merton in rather the same way that Yeats's acceptance of the invisible universe affected Lewis. He respected the man; he had never suspected a "religious" viewpoint from such a source; and that in itself shook him out of his own complacency.

But perhaps the strongest influence on Merton among all the people he knew at Columbia was the Hindu monk known as "Bramachari" who quite accidentally (or providentially) strayed into Merton's circle and showed him for the first time, and at close range, the change which the life of the spirit can work in a man. In Bramachari, Merton came up against holiness head on and it quite startled him. Up to that time, he had thought of religion as a system of beliefs, something one talked, professed, even expounded. In Bramachari, he perceived religion not as a viewpoint to be adopted, but as a life to be lived. An instance of the effect of Bramachari on Merton came in their first meeting. "We rode up to Columbia in the subway . . . and I was asking Bramachari about all the colleges he had been visiting. Did he like Smith, did he like Harvard? . . . I asked him which one he liked best, and he told me they were all the same to him: it had never occurred to him that one might have any special preference in such things."[12]

Up to that moment, Merton had no notion of such a thing as detachment. In Bramachari, he encountered it for the first time, not only as a concept, but as something concrete. It was an aspect of Bramachari's own pursuit of holiness. Startled by Bramachari's indifference to places, Merton "lapsed into reverent silence" and pondered on his own attachments, his cherishing of the idea of finding one particular place that would be "altogether pleasant to live and teach in." Bramachari showed him, just by this simple observation of his, the superficiality of his own approach. But I do not mean to be critical of Merton. He was shedding that superficiality as fast as he could. And he had a great openness to the holiness which he found in Bramachari. It was, after all, what he most longed for himself.

In Bramachari, Merton discovered what asceticism really was: not something which made a man gaunt and weak, but something which made him profoundly happy. Existing far from home in total poverty, entirely dependent on the good offices of others, and blown by the winds of fortune, Bramachari maintained a peace and calm like nothing Merton had seen before. He ate modestly; did not smoke or drink; prayed a great deal, and on a regular schedule; and went about his investigation of the United States and its curious cultural patterns with a sweet cheerfulness which Merton had not seen in a human being before. Merton saw for the first time that it was possible to be a monk and a happy man; indeed, knowing Bramachari, it was possible to suppose that monks were the happiest of men.

What was even more surprising was that Bramachari did not try to make a Hindu out of Merton. Instead, with charity and tolerance, he encouraged Merton to discover his own streams of Christian asceticism and holiness. He suggested that Merton read Augustine, observing that it was a pity that the Western world had so much abandoned its contemplative tradition. In particular, he recommended Augustine's *Confessions* and *The Imitation of Christ*. To Merton, this friendship, and this particular act of friendship—recommending him to his own spiritual tradition—seemed providential. In looking back on this moment, it seemed to Merton that God might have brought Bramachari all the way from India just in order that he might say these things. Yet Bramachari was only one of many influences beginning to converge. In doing work on his M.A. thesis, he came upon Mari-

tain's *Art and Scholasticism*, a book which not only helped him to
solve the problems he had set for himself in the thesis, but helped
him to his first appreciation of virtue. Through a combination of
influences including Maritain's intellect, Blake's insight, and Bramachari's example, Merton began to think of virtue as a way to
happiness, to harmony and perfection. For the first time in his life
Merton began to desire virtue and to want to dedicate his life to
God. "The notion was still . . . ludicrously impractical in the
sense that I was already dreaming of mystical union when I did
not even keep the simplest rudiments of the moral law. . . ."[13]

But through the influence of friends and writers most com-
pelling to him, he had made the first of many choices to be made
on the way to God.

Soon after this another impulse came, so strong that he could
not resist it: to go to church. He had been spending every Sunday
out on Long Island, visiting the same girl, but now, every week, as
Sunday approached, he found himself wanting to stay in New
York and go to Mass in a Catholic Church, something which, despite his visits to churches and monasteries in Rome, he had never
done before.

> First, there was this sweet, strong, gentle clean urge in me which
> said: "Go to Mass! Go to Mass!" It was something new and
> strange, this voice that seemed to prompt me, this firm, growing
> interior conviction of what I needed to do. . . . And when I
> gave in to it, it did not exult over me, and trample me down, but
> it carried me forward serenely and with purposeful direction.[14]

The experience was both strange and satisfying to Merton. He
felt in the church an atmosphere of prayer that quite surprised
him. And the sermon struck him as being what he most needed to
hear that day—a sermon which reflected centuries of unified and
consistent doctrine. Merton sensed the holiness of what he was experiencing, even though he couldn't understand it. But after the
sermon, as the central part of the Mass began, he became frightened and fled from the church. He did not go back the next Sunday. He was not yet ready for instruction, for baptism. But he was
caught in a process which he knew was gathering momentum—his

reading, his friendships, everything in his experience seemed to be leading in one direction.

The experience of being surrounded did not come to me primarily through friendship, as it did to Merton and Lewis. But I think it definitely came to me in a different way.

At this time in my life I had a passion for films and theater; they were more influential to me, I think, than most of the people I knew. I read plays, went to see them, had a stab at writing them. When I went to the movies, it was not just for enjoyment; I went to see the films as a way of understanding how other people saw the fundamental reality of things.

Oddly enough, it was the writers and filmmakers who were most distant from God who began to surround me with a sense of his reality. Many of the plays which were current then were of the absurdist school. They asserted, as an act of faith, that the world did not make sense and could not be put together in any coherent order. Perhaps the most striking of these plays was Samuel Beckett's *Waiting for Godot*. The two men were waiting forever in a senseless universe, completely bleak and without consolation, for a god who never came. *Endgame* was another example; there were dozens of others.

Somehow I felt that God was right there on the stage with them, but that through some quirk of vision—rather like a stage convention—they were ignoring the fact that he was there! I was rather like children in theaters who want to stand up and shout at the actors, "Look out, he's right behind you!" I could see God in the artistic brilliance which they were using to invent their empty universes; I could see him in their compassion for the sufferings of others; I could see him even in their denial of him. God was like the hidden pattern drawn into a picture of something else, the puzzle one finds in children's magazines. I would be looking at a play or a film which said how empty it all was, and I would see God even there.

I couldn't get over the feeling that people were shutting him out, not the other way around. An image in *La Dolce Vita*, a film by Fellini, seemed to say it better than anything. It was the moment when a helicopter flies over the city of Rome, carrying an enormous crucifix. But below it was a vast city where people were desperately seeking for pleasure, meaning, success—all the things they couldn't find. And something in me wanted to say, look up, he's right over there.

Admittedly, my sense of humor was a little off. When I saw films like *Tom Jones*—uproarious farces in which a charming rogue exploits other people and gets away with it—I didn't find them funny at all. They simply depressed me. And when I saw Robert Bolt's play *A Man for All Seasons*, I felt a sudden surge of hope. In this play, God seemed very real indeed. Even the characters who had not been faithful to him seemed to believe in him. And what a sharp contrast More presented to the anti-heroes in most contemporary plays. It was quite refreshing. Then I was assailed by my favorite doubt again: More belonged to the past; could there be such people nowadays?

Perhaps it was the very expression "nowadays" that confronted and challenged me most of all. I was on my way to belief; I was in the thick of the struggle. I could see God everywhere around me, even in places where human authors hadn't intended him. What was holding me back was "nowadays"—a clinging to the mentality of my own time.

But about this time I happened to read again some of the works of Oscar Wilde. There was no religious impulse in doing this; it was part of my constant interest in reading well-put-together plays, just to see what made them tick. And everywhere in Wilde's plays the word "nowadays" jumped out at me. The people in Wilde's plays were dominated by fashion; everyone was in a fever to do what was being done nowadays, to be approved of by everyone else. The word "nowadays" stood for a whole way of thinking and believing; and the world they had lived for had definitely passed away.

In reflecting on this, I began to think that I, too, had become a disciple of nowadays. I would not let go and give in to the Lord because he was not contemporary; his art and music, his churches —Father Moore in his cassock—all belonged to a time gone by; God was not relevant; he was not a fashionable idea.

What I needed was the courage to go by my own vision of reality; to face the fact that I would have to be, as Lewis once called himself, a dinosaur. Everywhere I looked at the contemporary scene where people were proclaiming that existence was meaningless; I could accept their view of the thing because they did, and be miserable with them; or else I could affirm another reality—more or less "by myself"—and be flung into churches populated by old folks and children; a way of life that wasn't stylish or avant-garde. Everything in my experience now conspired, somehow, to make me see how much the winds of fashion had been blowing me.

So in a different way from Merton and Lewis, I was surrounded, not by a crowd of friends going over to God and leaving me in the dust, but by the presence of God confronting me, even reproaching me, in the things I read and did and saw. These experiences seemed to me to be God saying, "Here I am, choose me, it's not nearly so hard as you're making it." But it was also clear that the choice would have to be made on my own, without the consolation of feeling that it was a fashionable thing to do.

But though I was not surrounded by friends and carried over the border into belief by them, friends did have an important part to play. I have already mentioned Father Moore and Stone Leake; but probably the most important Christian who came into my life at that time was a young man named Henry William Griffin.

I almost hesitate to mention him because I married him; and while that is in itself a marvelous thing, the fact of it often inclines people to assume that the religious choices I made were for the sake of marriage; and that was not the case. What Bill was to me then I remember clearly; one of the first intimate friends of my own age whose life was animated by his belief in God. I can't say that he caused me to be interested in Christianity; I was already taking instructions with Father Moore at the time I met him; but the friendship certainly shaped and formed a great many of my ideas about God.

For the sake of my story I would like to say that he had no influence upon my becoming a Catholic, but it really wouldn't be honest to pretend that. However, he did not pressure me; he did not make me feel "unsaved" because I was not a Catholic. Most of all, I didn't feel, once we came to see that we were falling in love, that that love was in any way contingent on our being of the same Christian denomination. When we talked about the faith, which we did a great deal, it seemed that we were talking about things we held in common, rather than things which divided us. And I think he was the first Roman Catholic I ever knew with whom I could talk about faith in that way.

And he was so joyful, so full of life and cheerfulness. Up to then, I had seen Catholicism as a dark cult of suffering and offering one's natural inclinations up. Bill made me think it was possible to celebrate life as a Catholic and a Christian. And that was very attractive.

Up to then, I had thought of Catholic belief as an enormously complex equation. One had to know a good deal about it; every doctrine was a matter of long tracts and pronouncements, with complicated distinctions that had to be made. Bill insisted that it was not nearly so complicated. He said (I am quite sure of this) that one only had to believe "about five things" to be a Catholic. (I have never quite been able to pin him down as to which five they are.)

But at the time when I first met him (when I was being instructed as an Anglican, and before I was baptized), the question of becoming a Roman Catholic had not even occurred to me. I was dealing with questions which are fundamental to Christian belief, not fine questions about the doctrines which separate Christians. And especially in my struggle with the question of the contemporary thinkers, Bill was an enormous help.

In many ways he was to me what Bramachari was to Merton. His grasp of religion made him dismiss lightly the things which seemed to me vitally important, such as the question of what city to live in. At that time I think I had some of the same ideas Merton struggled with in college days—among them a view that where you lived was somehow a kind of way to salvation. Should I be living in New York? Wasn't it really a wasteland of false values, filled with selfish, success-driven people? Bill seemed to think it didn't matter where you lived, that holiness wasn't a matter of living in a certain sort of environment. Should I be working in advertising? Wouldn't a teaching career be more virtuous, more significant for humanity? Bill thought the academic life was no guarantee of salvation, either. Most of all, he didn't seem to think it mattered what most of his contemporaries thought. He struck me as being a lot like Lewis in this way. He seemed to think that the question of what century you lived in was as irrelevant as the question of what city you lived in. He was impatient with Christian thinkers who tried to glorify one time or another as being especially Christian. The kind of nostalgia Chesterton and some other Christians had for a medieval world in which everyone was Christian did not make any especial appeal to him; he really seemed to like the modern world; at any rate he thought it was as possible to be a Christian now as it had ever been.

He even seemed to like being an American. Though he came from Irish forebears, he wasn't especially romantic about Ireland; he liked the thought that his Irish ancestors had pulled up stakes and come over here to make a new start. When I talked about Sartre and Camus and Simone de Beauvoir, the European thinkers for whom life seemed so bleak, he wondered whether Americans might not be more hopeful because we were a young country just starting out. But he wasn't naive about that: he knew America had its own share of trouble; his own father had experienced religious discrimination as a young man in Boston. Bill's attitude about America seemed more like a reflection of his fundamental cast of mind: a kind of hopefulness that didn't seem to be attached to times or places. It seemed to me that one source of his hopefulness was that he really believed in God.

As I came to know him well, I explored with him every possible objection I could think of, and it was then that I came to see how deep his faith really was. I can remember talking to him one day about biblical scholarship, and the possibility that, somehow, the story of Jesus might be shown, on good historical evidence, not to be true. What if the vast structure on which Christians have pinned their hopes were somehow to be undermined by some great sweeping discoveries in any realm?

And he assured me very quietly that he would believe in God

anyway. And when I asked him why, he answered: "Because of my own experience."

He had crossed the border, all right. He was definitely on the other side. He had made the leap that I was so hesitant about making. And just the fact that he had made it—and was a real flesh-and-blood person I knew—made me think that I could do it too.

Another thing I think I learned from him—though I could not say how—is that it was possible to pray. I do not say I had never prayed before this time. Undoubtedly I had, but usually it was a response to some kind of anxiety or stress. The prayer was often a hope-against-hope kind of prayer, flung into the universe without any real confidence that it would land anywhere. Perhaps Bill was the first person I had ever prayed with, and known that he was really praying. Prayers in churches (or so it seemed then) were things that people recited, sometimes very beautifully, but because the occasion demanded it; they were like invocations by clergymen when ships are being launched or bridges being opened. Bill took me into churches when there was nothing special going on; and we prayed there together, by ourselves. I think I began, through this experience of praying with him, to feel that the main reason for praying was not because you needed something, but simply because God was there. After a while, I began to be able to pray by myself, not only in churches, but at odd moments, alone in my apartment, when there was no special reason to do so. And there was a new kind of quietness in my prayer.

⌠ I come now to that embarrassing part of the Struggle which I must call the appearance of a sense of sin. I call it embarrassing only because, for so many modern people, Christianity is seen primarily as a religion of people who are guilt-ridden; who beat their breasts and hate themselves for what they have done and have not done. To outsiders, Christianity sometimes seems less a religion of ⌊love than one of self-hatred and self-abnegation.

But there is no way around sin when it comes to Christian conversion. The inevitable result of beginning to glimpse the immensity of God's goodness and power and love is to see at the same time our own unworthiness;⌡to gain a knowledge (which is sometimes overwhelming) of our own flawed nature, a nature which makes us desire virtue on the one hand, but behave unvirtuously on the other, almost it seems against our better judgment, against (as it were) our own will.

Lewis, in *Surprised by Joy*, only hints at this growing sense of his own unworthiness; in some of his other books he expresses it plainly. But Merton and Griffiths are not so reticent. They speak quite openly of their own sense of sinfulness: of their contrition and sorrow.

Time and again in *The Seven Storey Mountain*, Merton describes the selfishness in which he was becoming more and more enmeshed and which was making him more and more wretched. Merton does not enumerate his sins; but he clearly describes his own sense of sin, and his sorrow. And he says that the inner wounds caused by his sins and selfishness were causing him to bleed to death.

Lewis says that, to the outer world, these expressions of unworthiness, which Christians use, often sound like "the self-depreciation of a Chinese gentleman when he calls himself 'this coarse and illiterate person.'"[15] To outsiders, these statements sound either insincere, as though we are protesting too much, or else like a kind of self-hatred.

[But I think that for converts—indeed for all Christians—the acknowledgment of sin is not self-hatred at all, but the beginning of self-acceptance and (in the healthy sense) of self-love. The dialogue with God which begins with the confession of one's own failures is not depressing; it is liberating. At last, perhaps even for the first time, we have been honest with ourselves about what we are; and we have been honest with the one Person before whom there is no deception. Through this experience we learn what we are; and we open ourselves for the first time to becoming better than we have been. For to be a sinner before God is to be safe, to be understood, to be forgiven, provided that we are honest with ourselves and him, and truly sorry for what we have done.]Even in our first confessions as Christians (whether to our fellow believers or to God alone), we learn that God does not hate us for what we have done; it is we who have been hating ourselves for the guilt we could not admit; and now that we do so we feel a profound release and the cleansing power of God's forgiving love. We learn in this moment that God loves us better than we love ourselves; that he loves our honesty in bringing our sins to him; and that he wills us to do better, but not without offering us that supportive love which will make a new beginning possible.

It is well to remember that the Bible's word for conversion is repentance. Any real turning to the Lord is a turning away from sin. For converts, this repentance is often wrought with tears. When converts come at last to the Lord, they bring to him the sorrows not of a week or a year but of a lifetime. At times the sins they confess are so dark and hateful to themselves that they have never looked honestly at them, but have repressed even the memory of their own wrongdoing. And it seems they have repressed it—tried to pretend that evil was good—because of a kind of hopelessness and despair. Until now, they had not dared to hope that they could do or be other than what they have done or been.

Before I became a Christian this notion of confessing my sins was hateful to me. It was not a question of unwillingness to confess my sins before another human being; it was in fact an unwillingness to confess my sins at all. I could not admit myself to be a sinner.

And yet in some part of myself I knew that I was flawed: the good that I wished to do I did not; and the bad that I wished not to do I did; and in some recess of my consciousness I was profoundly ashamed. The confession which Christians make—have made since the earliest times—was for me (when I discovered it) a refreshing piece of honesty. It was a kind of release. And in doing so, I also found I had a great deal of company, which oddly enough gave me enormous hope.

The experience of private confession (which I came to much later on) held its terrors; but they were not greater (I think rather less) than the first terror of admitting my sins before God. But by then, looking on priests with eyes of faith, I had begun to see them not as men but as Jesus Christ himself; and I remembered with what tenderness he had dealt with tax collectors and adulteresses, with my own favorite among the saints, Mary Magdalene.

Contrition and sorrow are fundamental to the Christian life; as fundamental as joy. Each is a corollary of the other. And contrition brings its own high, its own sweetness, with faith: for with our contrition we put ourselves once again in the right relation to God. It is only while we are pretending that we have done nothing wrong—or that, if we did, we had a perfect right to do so—that our lives and hearts are askew and awry; once we have admitted what we are, a cleansing humility seems to flow into us; in confessing we make ourselves less, and the Lord makes us more: we are free and able to begin again, stronger, somehow, than before.

In some conversions, this aspect of the conversion experience is so pronounced that it seems to be the whole reason for the conversion. James, I think, makes it seem, sometimes, as though the experience of conversion were somehow a direct result of the convert's sense of failure: his misery is what propels him into the pursuit of virtue. There is some truth in this. Lewis speaks somewhere of people who come to Christianity in order to be cured of some habit such as masturbation, something which gives them an inward shame, for which they hate themselves and which they cannot overcome without the help of God's grace and the supportive life of the sacraments. But while a sense of sin is common to all conversions, I think conversion should not be confused with a mere effort to overcome bad personal habits.

Also, the sorrow which the sinner feels before God is very different from the shame which is felt by anyone at socially unacceptable habits. To continue with the example of masturbation: At least in our own era there is much to suggest that—speaking humanly—there is nothing wrong with it; and that the shame felt by some who masturbate (I dare say not all) is merely the result of pressure from prevailing opinion; while the sorrow felt by the sinner before God ought to be (and is) different in every way from this. His feeling of sinfulness is not because he has done something the world would disapprove of (indeed there are many sins of which the world would very much approve); instead the sin which he should sense is that of disobedience to his Father's will. And this sense of sin can come only when the Father is seen to be real; seen to be personal; and seen to be one who wills good for us even when we ourselves cannot see the good of his will, or accept it. It is only in this context that the law of Moses and of Jesus can be seen not as a set of arbitrary restrictions (as Dulles first thought, reflecting the values of a particular group in society) but as the necessity placed on us by reality; and that reality one of love. It is our growing sense of the Father's love, and that he is nothing but love, which makes us aware of how little we deserve what he has given us; that we are nothing but what he has made us; that we are his; and that our lives and our bodies are entrusted to us, not for our own use, but for his. In this perspective, sin is something quite different from what the non-believer may suppose it to be. It is not so much the fear of God which brings sinners to their knees; it is the knowledge of his inexhaustible forgiveness and love.

I touched earlier on Merton's very first experience of contrition. Oddly enough it was connected with an experience which might be called mystical or otherworldly. I say "oddly" because such experience was not characteristic of Merton's life up to that point nor of his habit of mind.

He was visiting Rome about a year after his father's death. He was alone in his hotel room with the light on when suddenly he became conscious of his father's presence—not from anything he could hear or see—but in a way he could not describe.

> The sense of his presence was as vivid and real and startling as if he had touched my arm or spoken to me. The whole thing passed in a flash, but in that flash, instantly, I was overwhelmed with a sudden and profound insight into the misery and corruption of my own soul, and I was pierced deeply with a light that made me realize something of the condition that I was in, and I was filled with horror at what I saw, and my whole being rose up in revolt against what was within me, and my soul desired escape and liberation and freedom from all this with an intensity like nothing I had ever known before. And now I think that for the first time in my whole life I really began to pray—praying not only with my lips and my intellect and my imagination, but praying out of the very roots of my life and of my being, and praying to the God I

had never known, to reach down towards me out of His darkness and to help me to get free of the thousand terrible things that held my will in their slavery.[16]

This incident took place before Merton began any serious consideration of Christianity. And in looking back on it, he is reluctant to place any great stress on the experience or make any claims for its authenticity. Could it not have been his imagination which made his father seem to be present at that moment? Merton is not sure. But he is sure that the experience was a grace. He regrets that he did not begin then and there to follow it through.

But he did begin, however falteringly, to pray. The morning which followed this incident, Merton went to the Dominican church on the Aventine, Santa Sabina. Up to this time Merton had always entered churches only as a tourist. This time he went straight to the altar rail and knelt down and said, "slowly, with all the belief I had in me, the Our Father."

This early incident in Merton's conversion is characteristic. His is a story of growing repentance. Over and over again he despairs of his own sinfulness; he longs to be cleansed and purified. But often his longing for virtue is not strong enough; he slips back into his old ways again. This is the whole pattern of the story he tells in *The Seven Storey Mountain*; even after he seizes on the pursuit of virtue at last, he is still struggling up a mountainside, making the steep ascent of Dante's *Purgatorio*, the purgative ascent of the soul towards God. And throughout his conversion, Merton feels a growing anger against, and disillusionment with, what he calls "the world." But the world which Merton turns against is not so much the world as it is a projection of the worldliness and selfishness which he found within himself. Once Merton had begun to struggle against his own sinfulness, once he had begun a life of holiness, he could revisit the same scenes which had depressed him because of their worldliness and see that what he had been fighting against was not the world at all, but "the world" within himself.

So there came in Merton's life, by fits and starts, a movement of the spirit which was beyond the intellectual consideration of faith; but instead it was a recognition of his own sinfulness and weak-

ness, a growing hatred of his sins, and a growing will to be freed
of them. But this took place over a long period of time, with
much indecision and procrastination and backsliding and hesitation. Yet it seems that throughout it all Merton had the grace to
pray, prayer that brought with it repentance. And that repentance
was not merely a temporary shame or regret, but a genuine movement, a turning.

Merton and Griffiths are alike in this: that long before either of
them became a monk, he tried to live like one. In Griffiths' case,
the efforts to live an ascetic's life began even before he was a fully
practicing Christian. Like Merton, Griffiths was troubled by the
modern world and deeply attracted by medieval spirituality. But
unlike Merton, Griffiths did more than dream about it. Together
with two of his friends at Oxford, he withdrew to the country and
tried to live in a rigorous monastic style. Without any direction
(not a recommended practice), he began to fast and undertake
other forms of austerity. And he found, as Merton did, that once
he did this he began to feel not deprived and wasted but strong
and alive and free.

But for Griffiths these efforts at prayer and asceticism were not
yet the full surrender of conversion. They were merely movements
in the struggle. The final resolution seems to have come in a
conflict which took place when Griffiths decided to spend a whole
night in prayer. As he describes it in *The Golden String*, it is very
reminiscent of Jacob's encounter with the angel with whom he
wrestled all night on the road. Jacob and the angel is in fact a
story of conversion; for in the morning, Jacob so fully accepted his
new relationship with the Lord that he was called by a new name:
Israel. Griffiths writes:

> Now for the first time I felt an overwhelming need to repent. I
> did not clearly understand what repentance was, nor was I aware
> of any particular sin of which I had to repent. It was simply that
> the unrest in my soul had turned from discontent with the world
> to a feeling of discontent with myself. There was nothing con-
> scious or deliberate about it; it came to me as a command, and I
> kept saying to myself, scarcely knowing the meaning of what I
> said: "I must repent, I must repent."[17]

Griffiths was staying as a guest in a London house, which had a small chapel at the top. He went there and prayed and, as he did, he formed a resolution (He says, "it formed itself in my mind") that he would spend the whole night in prayer. "Again," he says, "the resolution seemed to me to come not from my own volition; it was an instinct with the force of a command."

Once he had done this he returned to his room, knelt beside his bed, and began to pray. Immediately a grave mental conflict began. He thought of the absurdity of what he had decided to do; he thought of how ridiculous it would seem in the eyes of other people; he began to become afraid of the isolation which was developing in his life; but perhaps most serious of all, he was terrified by what seemed to him the irrationality of what he was doing; it was against all reason and common sense.

Up to this point, his consideration of religion had gone along entirely rational lines. His experiences of beauty and mystery in nature had been explained and made reasonable by the poets and philosophers he had been reading. His discovery of Christian teaching through philosophy and through "the ordered beauty of The Book of Common Prayer" had up to this point been completely rational. But now new irrational religious feelings were asserting themselves: the desire to fast, the desire to repent, the desire for extended prayer.

This conflict raged in Griffiths below the level of rationality. And he began to see how, in clinging to reason, he had been clinging to his own will: " . . . without knowing it I had made a God of my own reason. I had made myself the judge of everything in heaven and earth. . . ." Now this new and seemingly irrational call to repentance made him afraid because he had to move beyond the protective barrier of his own reason.

> Something had arisen in the depths of my own nature which I was powerless to control. I was being called to surrender the very citadel of myself. I was completely in the dark. I did not really know what repentance was or what I was required to repent of. It was this darkness which really made me afraid. Is not this the one thing of which we are all afraid? The darkness outside the

sphere of our consciousness, the abyss where all known landmarks fail?[18]

But Griffiths was determined to persist. He would not rise from his knees until the long night of prayer was over. Undoubtedly fear and fatigue magnified everything in his eyes. Yet it appears that he was coming to grips with the central conflict of his conversion:

> I do not wish to exaggerate the nature of this ordeal, but it was indeed the turning-point of my life. The struggle went on for many hours, but I realized at length that it was my reason I had to renounce. . . . I had to surrender myself into the hands of a power which was above my reason, which would not allow me to argue but commanded me to obey. Yet this power presented itself as nothing but darkness, an utter blank.

Every support, every protection was blasted and blown away. Griffiths felt desolate. He did not know where to turn. But instinctively he turned in the direction of the Lord:

> I had never been in the habit of meditating on the passion of Christ, but the scene in the garden of Gethsemane had impressed itself on my imagination. . . .
> Now I felt this hour had come upon me, and I could only place myself beside him in the garden of Gethsemane and wait for the night to pass.

This was more than instinctive. It was an action of the will, one requiring great control.

> Once I had made up my mind not to listen to reason, the conflict ceased. It was only a matter of enduring to the end. So I set myself to remain kneeling on the floor, fighting against sleep and keeping my mind fixed on the figure of Christ. Somehow I managed to endure until it was morning.

But when morning came, Griffiths felt tired and hopeless. He had persevered but felt no consolation. He did not know where he was heading or what would become of him next. Then an unusual thing took place.

> . . . as I was leaving the room, I suddenly heard a voice say: "You must go to a retreat." When I say that I heard a voice, I

do not mean that I heard any sound. It was simply that this was signified to me interiorly, but in such a way that it did not appear to come from myself.

From this experience and Merton's and mine, of voices heard but not with the external ear, it may appear that all conversions are full of such strange things. I cannot say what they are; nor can anyone, even those who have had such experiences, say what they are. They are promptings. One cannot account for them. Undoubtedly they can be explained as suggestions which our minds make to us in particularly real imaginative form. In fact, I do not now think it necessary to account for them; but only to know that for those who are entered into the spiritual life in earnest, such promptings do come, unpredictably, unexpectedly, and that when they come they seem like visits from angels.

So I do not intend to argue that the inner voice which Griffiths heard was any kind of intervention. But it is worth noting that at the time he heard the voice saying, "You must go to a retreat," he did not know what a retreat was. He had only a vague idea that it was some sort of a "clerical conference which I had heard of taking place in the country." In response to the inner direction, Griffiths was not quite sure what to do. But he went to a nearby Anglo-Catholic church and inquired if there was "such a thing as a retreat to which I could go." After a moment's consideration, the priest in charge responded that there was one beginning that morning at Westminster House for a group of men seeking ordination. Griffiths would be welcome to join them. Griffiths went there and learned that Westminster House was a community of Cowley Fathers. In attending the retreat conferences, Griffiths heard an old Anglican priest preaching on doctrines such as original sin, redemption, the Incarnation, and the Trinity. "This was the first time," he says, "that I had ever heard these doctrines expounded in a way which had any meaning to me." Despite his studies of philosophy, theology, church history and doctrine, "the simple truth of the faith had never before been set before me." At this moment, Griffiths felt that he had been exposed to the truths of religion but had turned his back on them. Now, this new insight into religious truths distressed him; it upset him to think he had never understood these things before. He felt as though he had been running away from the truth and was now brought back to the point from which he had started.

In this new context, the repentance for which he had been praying all night came to him at last. The retreat gave him the opportunity to make his confession, and he did so for the first time in his life.

> . . . tears poured from my eyes, tears of a kind which I had never known before. My whole being seemed to be renewed. When I went into the church and heard the chanting of the Psalms, it seemed that the words were being spoken in the depths of my own soul and were the utterance of my own prayer.

In this state of mind Griffiths saw everything about him heightened and transfigured:

> It was as though I had been given a new power of vision. Everything seemed to lose its hardness and rigidity and become alive. When I looked at the crucifix on the wall, it seemed to me to be a living person. . . . When I went outside I found that the world about me no longer oppressed me as it had done. The hard casing of exterior reality seemed to be broken through, and everything disclosed its inner being. The buses in the street seemed to have lost their solidity and to be glowing with light. I hardly felt the ground as I trod, and I think that I must have been in some danger of being run over.

When Griffiths returned to the house, he began reading the words of John: "Not that we loved God but that he loved us." This seemed the key to his whole experience: how, despite all his seeking, he could not find God, but now God had found him. That night before going to bed Griffiths read for the first time the words of John of the Cross which were to shape his life thereafter: "I will lead thee by a way thou knowest not to a secret chamber of love." He felt he could understand the meaning of love for the first time, and more than understanding it, he experienced it with great intensity.

It was as though a wave of love flowed over me, a love as real and personal as any human love could be, and yet infinitely transcending all human limitations. It invaded my being and seemed to fill not only my soul but my body. My body seemed to dissolve, as things about me had done, and felt light and buoyant. When I lay down I felt as though I might float on the bed, and I experienced such rapture that I could imagine no ecstasy of love beyond it.

What Griffiths is describing is of course an extraordinary experience of surrender in prayer. It is reminiscent of many such experiences which have been described by spiritual writers over the centuries; and it bears a great resemblance to some stories which William James includes in *The Varieties of Religious Experience* when he discusses sudden or instantaneous conversion. However, despite his surrender in prayer, Griffiths was still in the thick of the battle:

> When I returned home after this, I thought that all my troubles were over. But I found that they had only increased. The old passion for fasting returned to me in greater force than ever, and now a new trial was added. Whenever I tried to go to bed, the thought would come to me that I ought to stay up in prayer . . . but I was still terrified of doing anything which might be thought unbalanced. . . .

He feared the exhaustion of long prayer vigils; but if he didn't give way to the impulse, he felt guilty instead. Reading the lives of the saints, Griffiths became even more confused. Such practices of watching and fasting had been common with them, but nowadays they were no longer in common use. He resolved then to give up fasting, but this produced a new trial. When he was fasting, his reading of Scripture was "charged with meaning." When he abandoned fasting, the Bible words seemed to lose their meaning and his faith began to waver. After continuing this way for some time, reading the lives of the saints, and alternating between fasting and not fasting, he decided to make a new start, by going out into the country and living as a hermit. He did so with a definite hope that in a period of extended isolation and prayer he could discover God's will for him. And it was this action of his which eventually was to help him resolve the conflicts he felt and make a more complete commitment of his life to God.[19]

Much of what Griffiths experienced in his trial may seem neurotic to us. In fact, that was what Griffiths was most afraid of— that what he was doing was unbalanced and unhealthy. Another interpretation is that Griffiths was being called to a life he as yet only dimly knew about: a life of monastic prayer. His experience seems eccentric in twentieth-century terms (or at least in those of his own generation); but in the full perspective of Jewish and Christian history, there have been innumerable persons called by God in just this same sort of way. In a sense, what Griffiths was suffering from was the same thing that plagued Lewis, a feeling that the religious beliefs and practices of the past could not possibly be valid for the present. One perfectly good interpretation of what Griffiths experienced was that God was speaking as directly to him as he did to Samuel in the temple. But Griffiths as yet did not have enough faith to confront that call easily and calmly. Only through such faith do we begin to see that God does speak to some of us at some times and asks a kind of devotion which is out of the ordinary; and that it is not even necessary to call this summons "miraculous"; it can simply be recognized as real. Once such a level of belief is reached, a call such as Griffiths experienced—to love God at the heights of passion and devotion— does not seem so unbalanced after all. But as yet Griffiths did not have such faith; he had little Christian instruction; most important of all, he did not yet know that in the life to which he was being called, the monastic life, his behavior, which then seemed so eccentric, would appear as natural as sunshine and new-mown hay.

What characterizes the Struggle, then, is a growing realization of the truth of God's existence, and at the same time a last-ditch reluctance to accept him. It seems as though the nearer we come to the Lord, the more we sense his overwhelming power, the more we begin to believe that he is real, the more we resist him. C. S. Lewis describes this well when he speaks of being in his rooms at Magdalen, night after night, and sensing the steady approach of "him whom I most earnestly desired not to meet." Why do converts fear this encounter so? Partly it is because we feel our own unworthiness and are not consoled by reassurances that everyone else is just as unworthy as we are; we simply do not feel equal to the confrontation which is upon us. Also, I think, the tension comes in part from a knowledge, as with all great life decisions, that the encounter which is approaching will change us. And we are afraid of change. The status quo, however undesirable, even depressing, is a known. And the new experience—in this case a meeting with the Lord himself—is an unknown.

For some converts there is also a knowledge that a radical change of life-style will be required of us, and this becomes a reason for delay. This was certainly the case with Dorothy Day. She had contracted a common-law marriage with a man whom she very much loved, and who was very much opposed to religion. Yet, through the natural happiness of this relationship, she came to the Lord in a way that she had not been able to do before. Many times in her life she had experienced a religious call. In particular, when she was imprisoned in Chicago, she had called for a Bible and had drawn great strength from reading the Psalms. This seems, in retrospect, to have been a great grace. Yet, after her ordeal was over, she did not turn to the Lord, but consciously rejected him. And this was not the first occasion in her life when she did so. A child who had known religious joy, she nevertheless deliberately chose atheism over religion because of her identification with the poor and the influence of Marxist thinking in her life.

But in her relationship with Forster, and the pregnancy which followed, she found such great natural happiness that, even before she could be said to believe, she began to pray. She prayed not out of need but out of thankfulness for the blessings being showered upon her.

Pregnancy brought her a contentment and peace she had not known before, and from this happiness, prayer began to flow as part of the natural rhythm of each day. It does not seem that Day experienced the intellectual dialectic which was part of the conversion experience for Lewis and the others. Her reasons for denying God had been non-intellectual; and when she came to accept him it was through a kind of direct experience which was non-intellectual as well.

She had been drawn to religion in part because of the lives of the saints. Now, in her pregnancy, the saints assumed a special meaning for her. She began to use the rosary and to address some of her prayers to Mary. Even so, she was not fully able to believe, but was struggling to do so.

> I was surprised that I found myself beginning to pray daily. I could not get down on my knees, but I could pray while I was walking. If I got down on my knees I thought, "Do I really believe? Whom am I praying to?" A terrible doubt came over me, and a sense of shame, and I wondered if I was praying because I was lonely, because I was unhappy.

But when she walked, she was able to pray, and it made her happy. But even in these good moments, she experienced some conflict and doubt:

> Then I thought suddenly, scornfully, "You are in a stupor of content. . . . Prayer with you is like the opiate of the people." And over and over again in my mind that phrase was repeated jeeringly, "Religion is the opiate of the people."[20]

Yet, the more she prayed, the more she became convinced that she was praying not out of sadness or loneliness but in gratitude for her own happiness. And her relationship to her mate was blissful—except that he could not share her new interest in faith. He resented it and rejected it outright.

> . . . it was impossible to talk about religion or faith to him. A wall immediately separated us. The very love of nature and the study of her secrets, which was bringing me to faith, cut [Forster] off from religion.

Yet she felt sure that Forster in some way, without himself believing in God, was bringing her to do so. "His ardent love of creation brought me to the creator of all things. But when I cried out, 'How can there be no God, when there are all these beautiful things,' he turned from me uneasily and complained that I was never satisfied. We loved each other so much that he wanted to remain in the love of the moment; he wanted me to rest in that love. He cried out against my attitude that there would be nothing left of that love without a faith."21

As the months passed, Dorothy Day became surer that she would want her child to be baptized. Once her daughter was born, there was no doubt of this in her mind:

> I knew that I was going to have my child baptized, cost what it may. I knew that I was not going to have her floundering through many years as I had done, doubting and hesitating, undisciplined and amoral. I felt it was the greatest thing I could do for my child. For myself, I prayed for the gift of faith. I was sure, yet not sure. I postponed the day of decision.

But the more she came close to belief, the more she began to sense the struggle yet to come, between the natural happiness she already had and the loss which would follow if she chose the faith:

> A woman does not want to be alone at such a time. . . . Becoming a Catholic would mean facing life alone and I clung to family life. It was hard to contemplate giving up a mate in order that my child and I could become members of the Church. Forster would have nothing to do with religion or with me if I embraced it. So I waited.22

And she likens this struggle to the struggle of childbirth which she has just gone through:

> There had been the physical struggle, the mortal combat almost, of giving birth to a child, and now there was coming the struggle for my own soul. Tamar would be baptized, and I knew the rending it would cause in human relations all around me. I was to be torn and agonized again, and I was all for putting off the hard day.23

I think most converts confront the same kind of choice, but often it is not so concretely symbolized in terms of human beings. Merton, for example, was living a very worldly life, one which he was coming to hate, but which had a powerful hold on him. But he had no such commitment to a person as Dorothy Day had, to hold him, as it were, "in the world." Lewis was a bachelor, Dulles a college student; and, as we have seen, Griffiths, even during his period of struggle, was already living in a very unworldly style. But the choice is not really between worldly human commitments and unworldly spiritual ones. The choice is between following our own way, living for ourselves entirely . . . and following the Lord's way and living for him. As with every other phase of conversion, the Struggle is an inward movement: a tension between the Lord's way and our own which is the first such confrontation we have made in our lives. In a way, it takes us by surprise. Perhaps that is because, until now, we have followed our own way, without being able to imagine any other way to follow. When we observed the upright behavior of others, especially Christians, we assumed that their goodness came to them easily, was natural to them. It is only now that we sense there is a war on—between the Lord's powerful love which draws us and the love of self which shapes us more than we realized.

But there comes at last a moment when the issue can no longer be put aside. To converts, it seems that this moment is not of our own making. More than ever we know, as Lewis put it, that we are playing Poker, not Patience, as we had supposed. In *These Came Home*, a small book of essays by converts, Robert Ostermann, telling the story of his own experience, says this:

> There is a moment in every man's life, crucial to the definition of his destiny, which, if fled or passed by without decision, is irrevocably lost with all its opportunities; one of those rare occasions for a conclusive yes or no. . . .
> Such moments do not occur twice about the same event; . . . the gift is offered, in one or another disguise, and one has the opportunity of consenting or not. . . .

Perhaps not every convert can remember the precise moment when this occurred, but Ostermann can. He recalls how a short passage from Raissa Maritain's *Pilgrim of the Absolute*, an anthology of writings by Leon Bloy, made the passion of Jesus Christ especially vivid, and identified each man with the guilty Judas, "referring to our faults as being like spit in Christ's face." How many other people might have seen this passage, been offended by it, or leafed past it, untouched. Yet for Ostermann, at this moment, it was the crisis of conversion:

> There was the offer; and it searched out like a flame the only answer I had. At last I had met the Man face to face. It was not a meeting one could possibly ignore.[24]

I do not know (thinking of the infinite mercy of God) that Ostermann is right in saying that these moments come only once in a lifetime. But I am sure that when one comes to such a moment and knows it for what it is, one does not casually pass by.

To recognize such a moment, our hearts and our minds must be wide open. Then, and only then, can the convert be led from the Struggle into his own Surrender.

5

Surrender

Surrender is the real turning point of conversion. It is the moment after which, whatever happens, whatever ups and downs we may have, we know that we belong to the Lord. Our allegiance is given; it is committed; we cannot turn back. That is not to say that we may not slip, that we may not transgress, that we may not weaken. But in Surrender, something fundamental happens. After that, nothing is ever the same.

I have already treated one example of Surrender, as it were, out of turn. The experience of Bede Griffiths, described in the last chapter, is Surrender. It is Surrender, in the sense that we usually think of it: a giving of self which brings an experience of exaltation. In Griffiths' case the Surrender was so intimately linked with the Struggle that it is difficult to disentangle them. So, in his case, we have gotten somewhat ahead of our story. But not every Surrender is accompanied with such euphoria. For others, the experience is just as real, but it is accompanied instead with an absence of feeling. It is without consolation. It is a humbling, a being brought low, and brings with it, not the tears and floating sensations of a near-mystical experience, but instead a kind of passage through a dark alley, without romanticism, without beauty, without joy. It is a crossing made in utter faith. It is a step into the darkness, an encounter with the unknown, for which the only resource is trust.

Perhaps it is artificial to think of Struggle and Surrender as two different movements in the conversion experience. In fact, they are the same movement. The Struggle is a rising to the climax, and the Surrender its resolution. For some (Griffiths is an example) both experiences occur so close in time that it is hard to separate them. With others, the Struggle is of enormous duration, and then the crisis comes—leading to a moment of Surrender clearly differentiated from the Struggle which has just gone before.

Griffiths writes of the Surrender in terms of a metaphor used by the priest in the retreat he was attending:

> . . . Father Tovey had compared the action of grace to a small child standing over an open trapdoor into a cellar where his father is standing. The cellar is in darkness and the child can see nothing. But he knows that his father is there, and his father tells him to jump. That is what had happened to me; I had jumped into the darkness, and I had been caught in the arms of love.[1]

It is this movement—a jump into the darkness—which constitutes the Surrender. But not everyone experiences it, as Griffiths did, with a sense of consolation and love.

"There was no strain of music from within," C. S. Lewis writes of this moment, "no smell of eternal orchards at the threshold, when I was dragged through the doorway. No kind of desire was present at all."[2] In this experience Lewis found that what he must do is not "find himself" (as the popular psychologist sometimes counsels us) but instead relinquish himself, give himself away. The fugitive, the runaway, is asked to give himself up and come quietly. And if there is less sense of adventure about it than the great romantic converts (like Augustine) have led us to believe, it is because (at a time of seeming exhaustion and defeat) we sense that we are being recruited in a cause, and the terms of that service are not known. It is the fear, Chesterton says, of a "fuller sacrament and a mightier army." There is nothing in our past experi-

ence to tell us "what we are in for" now. "To a certain extent,"
Chesterton goes on, "it is a fear which attaches to all unknown
and irrevocable decisions. It is suggested in all the old jokes about
the shakiness of the bridegroom at the wedding or the recruit . . .
who gets drunk. . . ."³ But in what sense is the decision irrevocable? Only if we believe that God is really there and intends to
keep his part of the contract we are so reluctant to make with
him. So we feel exposed, unprotected: we are dealing with someone more powerful than anyone with whom we ever intended to
deal. We cannot hide or posture or dissemble. We have nothing
to wrap ourselves in but faith and that is a very thin covering.
And we have nothing to say but "Here I am. I come to do your
will."

I think one reason why others romanticize and beautify the
total surrender of conversion is that it appears from a distance so
very appealing and satisfying. Even converts themselves, looking
back on the experience, beautify it. For they can see in the perspective of what came after what a good and wholesome thing
that surrender was. But when you are undergoing it, to be
"dragged through a doorway" in a state of total submission has
more in common with the crucifixion than with what came after.
In the light of history and faith, Christians see the beauty of the
Risen Lord even in his dying on the cross. Yet, were one to have
been present as the cross was carried through the Jerusalem
streets, one would have seen only a humbling: a humiliation.

Of this final movement Chesterton writes: "There is a last second of time or hair's-breadth of space, before the iron leaps to the
magnet, an abyss full of all the unfathomable forces of the universe. The space between doing and not doing a thing is so tiny
and so vast." And this time, Chesterton says, is an "interval of intense nervousness," a time of fear. "If I may refer once more to
personal experience, I may say that I for one was never less troubled by doubts than in the last phase, when I was troubled by
fears." Those fears, he says, were of taking the step itself: "fears of
something that had the finality and simplicity of suicide." Yet,
"the more I thrust the thing into the back of my mind, the more
certain I grew of what Thing it was."⁴

The experience which Chesterton is here describing is an experience which is common to all the conversions which I am considering, including my own. Yet for each person a different turning point or event is the occasion for the last surrender.

Lewis, for example, experiences this surrender when he yields for the first time to the reality of God's existence. Chesterton is wrestling not with God's existence only, but with his acceptance of Roman Catholicism. For Merton, on the other hand, to become a Roman Catholic was only a step on the way, and a very incomplete step at that. His total capitulation came when he began to make fundamental changes in his own way of life and yielded at last to the call of priesthood and the monastic life. In each experience the individual is carried at last to the barriers of an enormous inward spiritual conflict: a conflict in which the central issue is known only to himself and to God.

[Speaking on conversion as a Jesuit priest and psychologist, John McCall defined conversion in these words: "(It is) giving up what you have—which is safe, secure and certain—for what you don't yet have—which is unsafe, insecure and uncertain—on the word of God and other people who love you." In developing this statement, McCall was elaborating from Newman: "If faith is the essence of the Christian life, it follows that our duty lies in risking upon God's word what we have for what we have not, and in doing so in a noble and generous way."[5]]

So there is a sense of risk which converts experience in this final moment. It is not yet a fear of the worldly consequences of the commitment they are about to make. It is not even a sense of the hurt they will cause to others by what they may do, nor of the wreckage it may effect in their lives, nor of the pain and cost of conversion in any worldly perspective. These things do hold the convert back, do cause him some grief and hesitation. But at this moment the sense of risk and danger comes from the Thing they are up against. It is the sense that they want for themselves (or have wanted up to now) to trudge along through experience, to procrastinate, to delay, to consider God and enjoy considering him without committing themselves to him. They sense, now, that this is no longer what God wants for them; that flirtation is ended; and that in fact he is telling them what he wants and that he wants nothing less than all.

"Total surrender," Lewis writes, "the absolute leap in the dark, were demanded. The reality with which no treaty can be made was upon me. The demand was not even 'All or nothing.' I think that stage had been passed. . . . Now, the demand was simply 'All.' "[6]

It is that all which can never be asked, fairly, by any human being, not mother, not father, not lover, not child. In our human relationships we are protected by the knowledge that no one can demand all of us, that we may and should keep something back, and that in doing so we are justified. Only one power in the universe has the right to ask that all of us; that power alone can ask it, and ask it fairly; and we wish in some part of ourselves that this all would not be asked. When the convert comes to know—as though for the first time, and all at once—that all is being asked of him and nothing else will do, that the all which is being asked will be defined by one who knows all of us, knows us more intimately than we know ourselves, he begins to be afraid that he cannot give that all, cannot make that deep surrender of himself which is against every human instinct of self-protection and self-preservation which he has. He is being asked to let go, to release control, to let God have his way; and to do this is to do something that he has never even thought of doing, let alone ever done, before.

There is still another reason for fear. In no human relationship, however dear or complete or fulfilling, have we ever known that deception was impossible. In every love affair on earth, we may pretend to give ourselves totally to others and know that in our inmost hearts we could still hold something back. With God no such pretense is possible.

"It follows," Newman said, "that our duty lies in risking upon God's word what we have for what we have not . . ." and McCall adds, "on the word of God and other people who love you." For whom on earth could we have such perfect trust that we could relinquish everything that is our own, our very selves? What sort of love assurances would we need from human beings in order to give our very selves away?

Only a perfect love could ask—fairly—for a perfect gift of self, an all. But the convert is asked to risk what he has for what he has not. He knows that his all is being asked, that a perfect gift and only a perfect gift will do. But he does not yet have the "what he has not"—the knowledge that God's love will perfect and magnify him through that very loss of himself and make of him what he himself could never be.

This, then, is the offer: Give up your life for me and I will give it back to you a thousandfold. Lose your life, to gain my life. It is a death that is being asked; a willing death; a death entered into with hope and trust.

Small wonder that a certain "nervousness" arises. Till now, we had not known (however much we had seen it in Scripture) that when God called us to a life with him, he would ask us first to die.

What a poetic notion, we had thought, when we saw it in St. Paul: "We who were baptized into Christ Jesus were baptized into his death."[7] Poetic, we had thought it, if we thought of it at all. But more likely we thought, Paul has such inscrutable forms of metaphor, such twistings and turnings of thought. Or then, when Peter and his brothers were asked to "leave all and follow me." Fishermen who dropped their nets to join the Lord's company seemed historical and quaint. They were not yet I; no such thing could be asked, we thought, of the me that is here and now.

"Now for the first time," C. S. Lewis writes, "I thought that (God) was out of reach not because of something I could not do but because of something I could not stop doing. If I could only leave off, let go, unmake myself, I would be there."[8]

The New Testament is full of it: the self that must be unmade before the real life can take hold, the death that must be died, in faith, before the resurrection can begin.

But what an act of trust is wanted here. The convert has not yet experienced, even guessed, what the love of God will be. Yet he cannot know that love until he has stopped clinging to the one thing on which he has pinned his whole security: himself and his own sense of dominance and control. He is the trapeze artist (it is

Kierkegaard's figure, I am told) who must let go of one swinging bar and reach across an emptiness until the next bar swings near enough. And the other bar, the one he is waiting for, is being swung towards him by someone he has not yet come to trust or know.

McCall uses another figure to describe this strange progress of conversion and love. It is of a man being taken, in stages, from a room which is familiar and comfortable, into a dark corridor, and then into another room which is unfamiliar and strange. The door is closed behind him and he must wait for the next to open. Yet, as soon as his familiarity with the new setting begins to give him comfort, he is called again into the dark corridor and brought to the next chamber. The path of experience with God is a progression from known to unknown, to known and then again to unknown.

How do converts know when this moment is reached? Suffice it to say they know, and they do not know how they know. It is a moment when all the arguments have been gone over with a fine-tooth comb; when the objections have been raised and dealt with as far as intellect and reason can; when many questions that have been raised are seen to be clearly unanswerable. It is a moment when all fears have been feared, all doubts doubted; when something within us says, If you are ever going to believe, it will be now.

The now is not only now. It is now or never. There is a sense that an invitation has been made, the banquet prepared; that the host has been infinitely patient for a reply. There is a knowledge, in the back of the mind, of those parables past forgetting, of how the reluctant dinner guest came later, only to find the great door closed in his face. There is the memory of the foolish virgins who went off to buy oil for their lamps and came back to find that the bridegroom had shut the door against them. There is the sense of a momentous chance given, and given not forever but in time. "For a game to be won," Lewis says, "it must be possible also to lose it." Now or never comes the call, and the call is clear. The convert may refuse it. But he knows that his refusal will be a definite, perhaps even an irrevocable, choice.

What a solitary moment this is. The convert is all alone in a place of his own making and knows all at once that Someone Else is there with him. That the Someone is invisible is merely to say that Psyche knew her lover only under cover of darkness; but she knew him to be real; knew that she had loved him when she could not see him; was afraid to look at him; and she knew that what was wanted of her was trust.

Trust, then, trust in the darkness, trust in the invisible, is the act of courage which the convert must summon up from the deepest part of his being.

Only after that step into nothingness will he feel about him the arms of love: a reality which he can know only by first believing it is real; a reality which he can experience only through his own act of faith.

Lewis does not speak of the aloneness of this moment. He does not speak of it as an anguish of decision or a burden of any kind. He speaks instead of a complete sense of freedom (not euphoric freedom, but freedom from necessity or compulsion, an ability to move freely one way or the other). It is this freedom from every sort of influence or gravitational pull from God or any other human being which gives such an unusual character to the actual moment of surrender. And this is completely consistent with what Christians suppose the reality of things to be. God who made us to know him and love him does not compel our love; will not exact our love as a price. For it to be love in a real sense, the gift must be given in perfect freedom. It cannot be demanded, or it ceases to be a love worthy of the name.

My own thought is that it is most like a child taking his first step or a young bird learning to fly. No amount of holding the child up and moving his feet in the proper sequence will accomplish the thing; it cannot be learned until it is done for the first time. A loving parent can provide example and encouragement, nothing more. Unless the child walks on his own he will not walk at all. Once on his feet, after the first few steps, he will catch on, will feel all at once that this is what he was always meant to do; but to do it, even when surrounded by well-wishers, he must do it entirely alone.

At a moment like this, pressure or coercion will only produce discouragement. So (in the light of Christian belief) it seems that God knows entirely how much at this moment our feelings need to be left alone. The island of stillness which comes at this moment—the moment Chesterton calls one of intense concentration —is exactly what the convert needs to make the decision which is before him.

Lewis expresses gratitude that at this moment he was so free of either desire or fear. He had no thought either of reward or punishment, and did not yet have any "sense of the promise of immortality." For Lewis, this was a good thing. "I had been brought up to believe that goodness was goodness only if it were disinterested, and that any hope of reward or punishment contaminated the will." If this was an error in his thinking, Lewis says, it was "most tenderly allowed for." He was afraid, he says, "that threats or promises would demoralize me; no threats or promises were made." Lewis found the commands "inexorable, but they were backed up by no 'sanctions.' God was to be obeyed simply because he was God."

Lewis likens this tender restraint on the part of God to his manner of dealing with the Hebrews, revealing himself to them without also making known the possible life hereafter. Lewis says of this that it was "among his greatest mercies." Lewis could then yield to God as the Hebrews had done, simply because of his recognition of the "I am." But Lewis had not learned to do this from the Hebrew Scriptures. Instead he had learned it "through the gods of Asgard, and later through the notion of the Absolute." To learn that God was to be revered not for anything he had done but merely for his existence was "a terror, but it was no surprise. . . ."

And so for Lewis, the surrender came at last: "You must picture me in that room at Magdalen, night after night, feeling, whenever my mind lifted even for a second from my work, the steady, unrelenting approach of Him whom I so earnestly desired not to meet. That which I greatly feared had at last come upon me." There was at last a moment of capitulation. "In the Trinity Term of 1929 I gave in, and admitted that God was God, and knelt and prayed; perhaps, that night, the most dejected and reluctant convert in all of England. I did not see then the most shining and obvious thing; the divine humility that will accept a convert even on such terms. The Prodigal Son at least walked home on his own feet. But who can duly adore that Love which will open the high gates to a prodigal who is brought in kicking, struggling, resentful, and darting his eyes in every direction for a chance of escape?"[9]

This moment of bowing the knee for Lewis came shortly after the moment which many regard as the actual turning point of his surrender, the moment of "totally free choice" as he went up Headington Hill on the top of a bus. This recollection of accepting God on a bus ride—like his memory of accepting the Incarnation while on the way to Whipsnade Zoo—reflects the humor which occurs throughout Lewis's most serious writing, and is, as Lewis himself said of Chesterton's wit, "not stuck in like currants in a cake, but the bloom on the dialectic itself." Lewis knew that sometimes our most heroic life choices are made in humdrum and homely situations. The humanness with which we make even our religious commitments reminds us, as Lewis observed of the sexual encounter, that we are "captive balloons," bounded in space and time.

Lewis seems to have complete recall not only of where he was but of how this moment of totally free choice felt to him. "I became aware that I was holding something at bay, or shutting something out." But Lewis felt that he was completely in control. "I could open the door or keep it shut, though I knew that to open the door meant the incalculable."[10]

Something very similar happened in the second episode on the way to Whipsnade Zoo. Yet these two episodes are not two surrenders but one. It seems from his account of the second, however briefly told, that Lewis was beginning to get the knack, if one may say it, of how such a spiritual crossing is made. The characteristics were the same. He remembers the same resistance, the same sense of shutting something out. But he says this resistance was not as strong as it was on the earlier occasion, and that once he had made the crossing, he could see it as a "further step in the same direction." In every other sense the two crossings are one complete passage: for in the first Lewis accepted God as God and in the second Jesus as Lord and Savior.

To identify this as the "last surrender" of Lewis's conversion may be misleading, however. It may suggest that something had ended without suggesting that at the same moment something had also begun; it might also imply, wrongly, that such a surrender is a resolution which removes all conflict and provides peace, certainty, freedom from doubt or care.

I hesitate to mention these wrong notions for fear of spreading them further, or confusing the reader. Conversion stories do end somewhere. But the conversion experience does not. It is taken up, like marriage after the wedding day, and lived in a different, perhaps maturer and more rewarding way.

It is interesting to compare the experience which Lewis describes with William James's discussion of "the psychology of self-surrender." For James, what happens at the crisis point of conversion is that the convert becomes so preoccupied with his own worries, fears, and anxieties that there are only two possible resolutions of the matter. One is that the opposite forms of emotion will spring up and suddenly reverse his course, which James thinks unlikely. The other is that he becomes so emotionally exhausted with his struggle that he stops everything: "so we drop down," James writes, "give up, and *don't care* any longer. Our emotional brain-centres strike work, and we lapse into a temporary apathy. Now there is documentary proof that this state of temporary exhaustion not infrequently forms part of the conversion crisis. So long as the egoistic worry of the sick soul guards the door, the expansive confidence of the soul of faith gains no presence. But let the former faint away, even but for a moment, and the latter can profit by the opportunity, and, having once acquired possession, may retain it. Carlyle's Teufelsdrockh passes from the everlasting No to the everlasting Yes through a 'Centre of Indifference.' "[11]

James, as we have already observed, conceived of conversion as a passage from unhappiness to happiness, from a negative emotional condition to a positive one. While it is hard to quarrel with his insights, not only because he is the grandfather of conversion psychology, but also because he documents so much of what he says from clinical or personal conversion experience, nevertheless I think he makes it seem too simple, as though a convert were changed from a person who is troubled and insecure to one who is at peace with himself and the universe, simply by the fact of accepting God into his life. The fact is that if a convert has certain neurotic dispositions—towards fearfulness and worry, towards anger, towards moodiness and depression—these psychological dispositions remain after conversion and must be dealt with as they were before. It is true that believing in God makes a difference; it makes it possible to begin the conquest of these negative feelings with a new confidence. But the conversion—which is a passage from unfaith to faith—does not automatically convert the emotions as well. What it does is provide a hope which the convert previously lacked: first, that the universe makes sense, and second, that it is possible to rely on God for help, when on his own he has been powerless to rule his destiny or his feelings. But the act of conversion is not the same as the fact of getting better. Conversion takes place only partly within the emotions, partly within the mind; and however personality may be defined, in whatever theoretical language, conversion is not the action of any one part of the personality but of the whole personality.

I sense here that I am getting into dangerous territory: I am verging on a psychological definition of conversion. I have not made any study of personality theory. I simply say that my own experience and that of the converts I know best suggests that we carry with us into the Christian life, bag and baggage, the whole array of natural dispositions, both good and bad, which we had before. What has changed is not ourselves but our view of ourselves and where we stand with relation to the rest of the universe. To the extent that the universe now seems to us animated with God's energy and life, shot through with his tender affection and love, we may be able to make a beginning in the conquest of despair, anger, irritability, unkind words and thoughts towards others, promiscuity, dishonesty, and other destructive habits of thought and behavior with which we have been struggling unsuccessfully up to now. But conversion is no guarantee of emotional well-being. Some of the holiest people who walked the earth were troubled with psychological trials and illnesses. It has often been argued that religion itself is an aspect of emotional imbalance! Yet we have also seen that, in lives filled with trial and difficulty, those who have turned to God rather than to themselves draw courage and resolution and perseverance from this turning. Perhaps I think that the idea that belief in God is a panacea for emotional ills is, as Lewis felt of immortality, an unfair inducement. If God is God, he should be acknowledged just for that; not opted for as a form of personal self-improvement!

But perhaps I am quarreling too much with James. Undoubtedly many of the cases which he drew on for his insights were of those who felt, once they had found God, their troubles were now over. James writes a good deal of what we should now call "evangelical born-again experience"—an instantaneous conversion surrender, sometimes accompanied by visions and illuminations, quite unlike the experience of Lewis and the others to which I found so many personal parallels. Even so I think James fully understood the dynamic—if such a term can be used—of surrender, the letting go of this final passage; he saw in it a recognition by the convert of his own inadequacy, his inability to save himself, by himself (though here "save" is my own term, not James's). James quotes this passage from the conversion account of David Brainerd, whom he calls "that genuine saint":

> One morning, while I was walking in a solitary place as usual, I at once saw that my contrivances and projects to procure deliverance and salvation for myself were utterly in vain; I was brought quite to a stand, as finding myself totally lost. I saw that it was forever impossible for me to do anything towards helping or delivering myself, that I had made all the pleas I ever could have made to all eternity; and that all my pleas were in vain, for I saw that self-interest had led me to pray, and that I had never once prayed from any respect to the glory of God. I saw that there was no necessary connection between my prayers and the bestowment of divine mercy; that they laid not the least obligation upon God to bestow his grace upon me; and that there was no more virtue or goodness in them than there would be in my paddling my hand in the water.

Brainerd is thus up against the Thing which Chesterton describes, the Thing which Lewis and Dulles and Merton felt as a power beyond powers; and he is overcome with sorrow at his own self-interested efforts to merit the grace of God, ashamed at his own pridefulness in assuming he could make demands on God by behaving in appropriate and deserving ways. He is on the brink of capitulation; but remorse is not yet surrender.

> I continued, as I remember, in this state of mind, from Friday morning till the Sabbath evening following (July 12, 1739) when I was walking again in the same solitary place. Here, in a mournful, melancholy state *I was attempting to pray; but found no heart to engage in that or any other duty; my former concern, exercise and religious affections were now gone, I thought that the spirit of God had quite left me; but still was not distressed; yet disconsolate, as if there was nothing in heaven or earth could make me happy.*

Having continued in this state for about half an hour, Brainerd was then favored with a burst of consolation: "an unspeakable glory," he says, "seemed to open to the apprehension of my soul."[12]

The passages which James italicizes in the Brainerd account do bear a definite resemblance to the experience of surrender in conversion, though they are far more emotional than any experience described by Dulles or Lewis; Griffiths and Merton experienced highs and lows such as this; perhaps it is a matter of the individual's nature and his willingness to disclose that experience. Brainerd's account is also an experience of surrender in prayer. Perhaps it is foolish to try to distinguish between conversion surrender and prayer surrender: both are acts of complete submission. Suffice it to say that the crisis of conversion can only be properly and fully resolved by a letting go, an unmaking of the self, which seems to be accompanied by a moment of total spiritual exhaustion. "You do it, God, I can't go another step on my own." In this moment the convert realizes how hard he has been trying to be God, to do it on his own; alternatively, he may realize, in the same moment of self-understanding, how hard he has been trying not to let God be God; not to let God into his life at all.

It seems then, both from the highly colored and visionary accounts of conversion and from the more sober and intellectually reasoned ones, that there is an ultimate moment of yielding. Lewis says it reminded him of snow melting. And it seems that this does not take place until the convert somehow gets beyond wanting, beyond his own efforts and demands, into a state where he wants nothing or cannot say with any clarity or confidence just what he wants. At this moment when he wants nothing, he is able to will something—but dispassionately: in Milton's phrase, "all passion spent."

In each conversion there is a surrender; but in each life it is associated with a different event. When Chesterton writes of the experience, he is telling not of his surrender to belief in God but to the Roman Catholic Church. For some years Chesterton had already been a believer; he had summarized his beliefs in a book which he called *Orthodoxy*, a "merely Christian" book, in Lewis's sense, stating traditional Christian doctrine in modern language. At the time of writing *Orthodoxy*, Chesterton was surely a converted man; yet a further movement and a further surrender was yet to be made. Perhaps the surrender which Chesterton made came first doctrinally, in the giving of his intellect to the Creed, and was only completed in the sacrifice of himself which came about in his conversion to Catholicism. With Merton, on the other hand, acceptance of Catholicism, his entry into the Church, was not yet the full surrender of his conversion, in the sense of a full and complete response to the call which he felt. Instead it was his acceptance of the call to priesthood and the monastic life.

Merton does not identify the moment when he did this, at least not in so many words. But in reading *The Seven Storey Mountain*, it seems to me quite plain that this occurred at a very definite moment in his life.

It came after a night like many other nights Merton spent with his college friends: a night of going to bars and drinking and staying up till 4 A.M. "because we couldn't think of anything else to do and there seemed to be no point in going to bed." The group of friends went back to Merton's apartment and slept there, some on the floor, some in chairs, some on uncomfortable couches.

Merton reflects that they were accustomed to discomforts of that sort, endured for the sake of an evening's pleasure, but would have been outraged at the thought of being uncomfortable for penitential reasons.

The following morning, as the group sat around playing records and having breakfast and smoking, the thought came to Merton very strongly that he wanted to enter a monastery and become a priest. Out of the blue, he found himself telling the others of this intention.

He walked one of his friends, a girl named Peggy Wells, to the subway and found himself telling her again that he was going to become a monk and a priest. She tried to be sympathetic and interested, but Merton could see it didn't make very much sense to her.

After that he was glad to be alone. He spent the rest of the day turning the thought over in his mind, and it became more and more real to him. After having supper at a little German bakery, he headed to St. Francis Xavier Church at Sixteenth Street. The church was locked, but he noticed a small door in the basement and found it open. There was a Holy Hour in progress: the Blessed Sacrament was exposed on the altar. He turned his eyes to the Host.

"And then it suddenly became clear to me," Merton writes, "that my whole life was at a crisis." Everything now seemed to be hanging on his decision, though up to that point nothing, he says, had been further from his mind. "It was a moment of crisis . . . and during that moment my whole life remained suspended on the edge of an abyss. . . ."

It was a moment of interrogation: "Do you really want to be a priest?" The hymn was ending. The moment was beginning to feel like a last chance.

"I looked straight at the Host, and I knew now who it was . . . and I said: 'Yes, I want to be a priest, with all my heart I want it. . . . If it is your will, make me a priest.'

"When I had said . . . those last four words . . . (I realized) what power I had put into motion on my behalf, and what a

union had been sealed between me and that power by my decision."[13]

More than any other turning Merton describes in *The Seven
Storey Mountain*, that one seems to me to have been decisive.

In my own case I find it hard to say which of the two surrenders I made was in fact the definitive one of my conversion. The
first was undoubtedly at Baptism, a surrender so remarkable and
total that I could not then imagine (nor can I now) that any action ever in one's life could ever be more decisive or complete. I
approached that sacrament with a full knowledge of its meaning
and with enormous gratitude: there was so much on my conscience then that I felt grateful, by force of circumstance, to be
coming to this immersion in the Lord so late in my life.

In becoming a Christian and an Anglican, I intended to make a
full surrender of myself to the One Holy Catholic and Apostolic
Church. What pain it gave me, shortly after, to discover that, in
spite of the spirit in which I had undertaken this sacrament, and
the joy with which Father Moore and Bishop Chambers had received me into the Lord, I was not able to rest in the place they
had made for me. At the moment of my Baptism, I was utterly
confident that in becoming an Anglican I was becoming a Catholic; and it was Catholic I wanted to be. Soon after that, issues of
an intellectual nature which I could not resolve made me feel that
my passage was not complete, that I had another distance to go.
However much I tried to resist these thoughts, to see them as
scruples arising from overly fine distinctions, or as temptations,
I could not put them aside. I saw all the sins and defects
of the Roman Catholic Church throughout the centuries, all its
arrogance and pride; but beyond that I could see clearly the shining beauty of the Body of Christ. Looking back at Father Moore,
at Bishop Chambers, at the other Anglicans and sincere Protes-
tants I knew, I felt they did not see the Church of Rome as I was
seeing it: I saw a radiance, a brilliance that blinded me. I wanted
to be there.

Once I knew this, I felt a real sorrow. I knew I would have to be
separated from loving friends in Christ, some of whom I had just
come to know, but with whom I felt a very special bond. I

thought of the pain and shock it would cause to my family. They had already endured the pain of a baptismal service which looked to them for all the world like a Roman Catholic rite. Hadn't I distressed them enough? Was it necessary to inflict the further pain of becoming a Roman Catholic, with all the abjurations and promises and denials and professions that would entail?

But I think the greatest part of my sadness was in feeling that we were all members of Christ's Body but that his body was somehow broken, and by us. It was our quarrels and transgressions that had made the divisions in Christianity, and I could see that no one was blameless in this. But a growing devotion to the Eucharist—and to a belief in the Real Presence—drew me into Roman Catholic churches. There the Blessed Sacrament was always kept for the prayer of the faithful at any time. In Anglican churches, only "high church" congregations observed this practice. So, in all of Manhattan, I knew only two Anglican churches in which I could find the Blessed Sacrament reserved. In Roman Catholic churches the Blessed Sacrament was always there. Doctrinally, the Anglicans, the Lutherans, and the Roman Catholics were one in believing in the Lord's Real Presence in the Eucharist. But the actions proceeding from this were different. As my devotion to the Eucharist grew, so did my attraction to Roman Catholicism.

I began now to attend both the Anglican and Roman Catholic churches on Sunday—an action symbolic of the conflict I felt—and I continued to do this for many weeks. It was not an easy matter to resolve. In the beauty of the Anglican high church liturgy (bells, vestments, elevation of the Host, and the prayer book language I so loved) I was totally at home, while in Roman Catholic churches I was a stranger. Though I knew Latin, it was impossible to follow the Mass without reading it in a book. In this time before the Second Vatican Council, large parts of the Mass were said in secret and could not be heard by the congregation. I was troubled by the giving of Communion only under the form of bread, while the reception of the wine was reserved for priests alone. All the Protestant charges about a high-handed, condescending, and proud hierarchy—reveling in its own show of pomp and circumstance—seemed to me thoroughly justified. Gradually, I began to understand (what was incomprehensible at first) the deep devotion of Catholics at Mass. But at the beginning, the rattling of rosaries and the saying of private devotions while the Mass was going on, not to mention those praying to saints at side altars while Mass was being said, seemed to me difficult to endure. It seemed to me a foreign church, neither English nor American in spirit. So my cultural roots held me back, as well as a thousand Protestant difficulties. At the same time I could not leave the issue alone. I could not rest as an Anglican; I could not yield to Rome. I continued in this miserable situation for some time.

At this particular turning of mine the authors who became most meaningful to me were Chesterton, Ronald Knox, Newman, and of course Bede Griffiths. Each of them had made a dual passage. First they had experienced conversion by a complete assent to the Lord within the Church of England. Then their perceptions had changed and they had made still another passage into the Church of Rome.

How, eventually, and on what fine points of difference between the Anglicans and the Romans I made my choice, I do not intend to say here. To do so would be foreign to the spirit of Lewis and of mere Christianity, which I think the only sure way for Christians now. Like Lewis, I think that we as Christians have much more to unite us than to separate us; and I think it is counter to the spirit of Christian unity to argue that every Christian, if only he could see it, is on his way to Rome.

I only know that in my own case it became clear at last that this was the particular path the Lord wanted me to follow. Once I had seen that, and believed it, I could not deny him. For this second surrender, a special grace was needed, and given.

I will never forget the special terror I felt when I left my desk one winter's evening and walked across Madison Avenue and went up into the massive structure opposite St. Patrick's Cathedral, which then symbolized for me everything institutional and forbidding about the Roman Catholic Church. What was I so afraid of? I had chosen the priest because I thought he was approachable, easy to talk to, Father Patrick Sullivan, a Jesuit, and I now find him fairly unforbidding to know. The terror perhaps, as Chesterton says, was of the Thing itself.

But I felt, too, what Merton felt on his way to Father Ford: resolution. I knew what I was doing and where I wanted to go. By this time the only question was how I was going to get there across an obstacle course of objections large and small that somehow had to be dealt with.

The wounds of that crossing—for myself and my family—have healed long ago. Indeed, it was worse to think about than to do. Much of the sadness that came into my family relationships at that time was caused by misunderstanding of the way in which my choice was being made. Once others came to understand how free and personal my decision was, they accepted it with understanding and with love.

So I think in my own case the surrender came when I knelt at the altar rail in St. Francis Xavier Church and swore on the Bible I had come to love so dearly to accept all that had been defined and declared by all the Councils of the Church including the Sacred Council of Trent.

I did so in the evening, with three dear friends as witnesses; after which I made a general confession for the second time in two years (having done so first at the time of my Baptism). And in the morning I received the Eucharist as a Roman Catholic for the first time. In the confidence that followed these actions I knew that my conversion was complete.

Looking back on that moment, it still seems to me charged with meaning, as though it represented the most fundamental choice I have ever made. Not just to believe in God. Not just to acknowledge him. Not just to live a good life in the best way I knew how. But to accept the idea that in my encounter with the Lord, there would be definite things that he would ask me to do, and that they would not always be easy. And to know that once I knew who was asking, I would answer yes.

So I would say that the surrender is not only a moment of self-giving; it is a moment of recognition which takes place in the most intimate, unexplainable way.

In a film called *Lili*, there is a scene which is for me a metaphor of this kind of recognition of the Lord. The film concerns a young woman who loved a puppeteer, but was never able to perceive his love for her. At the last, when she is preparing to leave the traveling circus, he speaks to her through his puppets; they tell her of their love. She returns and speaks to the puppets as though they were alive. It is only after a few moments that she knows it is not the puppets who are speaking, but the puppeteer behind the curtain, who is giving them life. I think the Surrender is this same kind of mutual recognition. The Lord has expressed his love to us through human beings and through events; but we have not been fully able to perceive his love until this final moment, when we can say, "My Lord and my God."

It is like Roxanne's final recognition that Cyrano has been her lover for a lifetime, though she had known him only in disguises and mediated through the love of others; now she sees that it was his love that shaped her life from the beginning, and she says, "It was you, and I might have known every time I heard you speak my name."

My recognition of the Lord in Surrender was like that. It was knowing that his love was not only mine then, but had been mine all along. He speaks to us, as Cyrano did to Roxanne, "in such a voice as I remember hearing long ago . . ."[14] and we know suddenly that the love is a mutual love. Not that we loved God, but that he loved us; loved us then when we could not understand it and now when we can understand it; loves us with a love that is passionate, tender, and personal.

6

Afterwards

I want to speak now of what happens afterwards, both the immediate results of conversion, and the way that conversion continues in the Christian life.

Those who are newly converted may experience at first a burst of thankfulness, even a kind of euphoria, a spontaneous charity for everyone and everything. I wanted to shout from the rooftops! No one has described this feeling better, I think, than Charles Dickens in writing of the conversion of Ebenezer Scrooge:

> The chuckle with which he (spoke) and the chuckle with which he paid for the turkey, and the chuckle with which he paid for the cab, and the chuckle with which he recompensed the boy, were only to be exceeded by the chuckle with which he sat down breathless in his chair again, and chuckled till he cried.

On finding himself alive, converted, and able to mend his ways, Scrooge had what we would call a peak experience:

> He went to church and walked about the streets and watched the children hurrying to and fro, and patted children on the head and questioned beggars, and looked into the kitchens of houses and up to the windows; and found that everything could yield

him pleasure. He never dreamed that any walk—that anything—could yield him so much happiness.[1]

I can recall thinking, in the first days after conversion, "Why doesn't somebody tell people about this?" It seemed to me I had been entrusted with an enormous secret, one which really ought to be shared. The instant I thought this, I knew, as Griffiths did, how often it had been told to me when I had not been able to hear it. So I felt as though I had been given a special grace. The ears of the deaf had been opened, and the sense of miracle was profound.

But this euphoria—which accompanies so many great and positive life decisions—cannot last for long. The day-to-day realities crowd in; the celestial music dies away; the energy which has been set loose within us has to be integrated into life in some practical way.

There are first of all practical choices to be made about how to manifest a Christian commitment in one's life and behavior; these choices are far from easy. One example is the need to turn what has been mostly a private dialogue with God into a real commitment to communal worship. For some, this change is painful.

Lewis, for example, never found churchgoing a satisfactory experience. He complained that it was difficult to pray in church, especially on weekdays, when the cleaning women with their mops and pails might disturb his private devotions. And on Sundays one always had to contend with hymn singing and vestibules full of umbrellas. Dulles and Merton and Griffiths were more fortunate in this regard. Merton became a Cistercian and found the life-style and its austerities precisely what he most needed then; Dulles entered the Jesuit order; Griffiths became a Benedictine monk. The liturgical style, in each case, was consonant with their own private spirituality. However, Griffiths had some adjustments to make; he found, once he had entered the monastery, that the life-style there was less austere than the one he had been practicing privately. In the monastery he had to get used to the heat being turned up too high.

For some converts there is an experience to be undergone which

I can only call "wreckage." It is the inadvertent damage done to the fabric of one's personal relationships by a conversion: an action which seems like a betrayal to those left behind. By her conversion, Dorothy Day cut off the most intimate relationship in her life. Gerard Manley Hopkins incurred the sharp disapproval of his parents, who had asked him to delay his reception into the Catholic Church for a year; he found himself unable to do so. John Henry Newman, a very public priest of the Church of England, caused a storm of anger and anxiety by his decision; this engaged him in no end of explanations, defenses, and controversy. Elizabeth Ann Seton and Cornelia Connelly, both converts to Roman Catholicism, became social outcasts within their own circles. This wreckage—the loss of affections or of position within the world—is a price which some converts pay for the course they travel. Though it is hard to see it in the context of his popularity today, C. S. Lewis also experienced such rejection because of his Christian commitment. While he had not done anything socially unacceptable, his vigorous defense of Christian orthodoxy made him unpopular with many of his colleagues at Oxford. In part, this may have been due to the rough-and-ready wit with which he destroyed many opponents in debate. Reflecting on the difficulties of the Christian apologist, Lewis remarked that he was never less sure of a doctrine than when he had just successfully defended it. In one of his poems he speaks of the inward tensions which this experience sometimes caused him:

> From all my lame defeats and oh! much more
> From all the victories that I seem to score;
> From cleverness shot forth on thy behalf
> At which, while angels weep, the audience laugh;
> From all my proofs of thy divinity,
> Thou, who wouldst give no sign, deliver me.

And he asks:

> Lord, of the narrow gate and needle's eye
> Take from me all my trumpery lest I die.[2]

But over and above the pique others may have felt at Lewis's style of argument, there may have been another reason why Lewis was passed over by his colleagues for the academic advancements which seemed due to him. When a conversion takes place, others may feel rejected. In *The Four Loves*, Lewis describes the resentments which may be felt in a family when one member develops a new interest the others do not share. Lewis here is describing just what he felt when his friends "went over" to religious belief. In Lewis's case this had the effect of inviting him to follow (not at first, but in the long run). It provoked him to examine Christianity as seriously as they had done. I too felt this almost envy of committed believers I knew. But the opposite effect may also occur. The convert's behavior may be seen as immature, egotistical, a kind of showing off, or as Lewis puts it, "swanking." It looks like affectation. This misunderstanding by his friends or family offends the convert in turn. Wounds of this sort are slow to heal. To make matters worse, the convert is not always joyfully welcomed by the community of believers. They experience a kind of resistance at the convert's approach. They are the ninety-nine who have been left to shift for themselves while the Lord went off in pursuit of this particular one. Those who have been Christians all along may even be wistful about the new convert's zeal. Born into the faith, raised in it from the cradle, they imagine they can never have the special experience of salvation which has been given to this new arrival. They have a little difficulty making room for him in the pew.

In my own case, I have found this resistance least, in fact completely absent, with those who, born into the Christian faith, have themselves experienced conversion. Chesterton is quite wrong, I think, in saying that the experience of being converted "from outside" is fundamentally different from the faith-awakening of those born into the faith. It may be true, as Chesterton suggests, that outsiders coming in have a greater sense of rescue, of being saved from themselves and their own natural inclinations. But I am not even sure about that. A more likely explanation, I think, is that many committed Christians are shy about speaking of their own personal encounter with the Lord. When we find those who are willing to do so, we find people who, like ourselves, have felt a sense of being personally called by God. At first, after becoming a

Catholic, I felt I had had an experience of Catholicism which could not be shared. But, as time went on, I heard others— Catholics from childhood—speaking of their own relationships with God (and sometimes proclaiming it *without* speaking of it) in ways which showed me how much they had experienced conversion, perhaps even more deeply than I had. I have had this same experience with Christians of other denominations, converts-in-place, so to speak, practicing the Christian faith they were born in. They are authentic converts. And in meeting each of them I have felt just what Lewis describes as the first spark of friendship: "What, you too? I thought I was the only one."

I think, too, that the zeal of converts-from-outside can become tiresome when it issues in talk and efforts to convince others, rather than when it results in genuine Christian behavior. Griffiths put a serious strain on his relationship with Lewis when he tried to explain his reasons for becoming a Catholic; they had shared the experience of discovering Christ, but debate about points of doctrine was another matter. Merton says that after he became a Catholic he loved to sit around at parties and talk theology, but had made few real changes in his way of life: "I was already dreaming of mystical union when I did not keep even the rudiments of the moral law." The new convert needs to resist the temptation to be argumentative or to bask in the glamor of the experience he has had. Even the slights and wounds which come to him at this time should be received with humility, made little of.

But wreckage and other practical problems of adjustment are not the most serious difficulties for the new convert. First of all, these problems are not, in general, enduring. Secondly, they are dramatic—they continue the high excitement of the conversion. They feed the ego! There comes a day, for some sooner than others, when the sense of an extraordinary event begins to ebb, a day which is as humdrum and unexciting as the days before conversion began. At this moment, the convert may have a rude awakening. Until now he has had the pleasure, the specialness, of coming late into the vineyard and learning that he would receive the same wages as the other workers. Now he finds himself where every other Christian is. The religious enthusiasm of the surrender wanes. The spiritual duties he has taken on feel once again, or for the first time, like burdens. What is more distressing, the convert finds that while he is a new man in Christ, he has brought over a good deal of the old man with him. His little sins and temptations begin to creep back into his life and catch him unawares.]He is still inclined to pique, even to anger; may still be jealous of a neighbor's good fortune; unloving to others; given to self-pity and despair. A round of distractions and doubts begins.

Avery Dulles expresses it this way:

> Having become a Catholic, I was surprised to learn that my conversion had scarcely begun. I had previously imagined that I would embark on a heroic course of action. . . . In this I was wrong, totally wrong. One's human nature remains, and with it all the tendencies of pride and selfishness which faith condemns. . . .

Dulles goes so far as to enumerate his sins and offenses:

> My natural sentiments are almost completely unbaptized. When I am insulted, anger and indignation rise within me as strongly as they did before. When delayed, I am impatient. When treated unjustly, I revile and do not bless. The most ordinary works of mercy, such as giving to the poor, visiting the sick, counseling the doubtful, are irksome to me. If I do them at all, it is in a half-hearted and ungenerous spirit which renders them practically worthless. Any heathen with a spark of natural goodness can put me to shame in matters of tact and human warmth. When it comes to the most elemental acts of public devotion, I am so embarrassed to appear different from others that it is a painful effort to bless myself even at meals. . . .[3]

I think this little confession which Dulles makes at the conclusion of A *Testimonial to Grace* is a good instance of what happens to converts "afterwards." With all their high hopes and dreams, with all their fantasies of goodness, they come up against the hard reality of human nature. No single act of faith, no first fervor is going to change all that. It is hard to accept the fact that the virtuous life is not suddenly acquired, but is a slow process of growth. Karl

Barth, in writing about conversion, says that the new man does not supplant the old man within us, but that they coexist throughout our lives in a constant tension. The mature Christian accepts this duality as something he will experience throughout his lifetime. But to the new Christian, the raw recruit, it is cause for discouragement.

In *The Screwtape Letters*, Lewis provides us with a good insight into this letdown after conversion by letting us see it from the Devil's point of view. Screwtape writes to Wormwood:

> Work hard, then, on the disappointment of the anticlimax which is certainly coming to the patient during his first few weeks as a churchman. . . .

Screwtape mentions to Wormwood a particular kind of obstacle which surely must have been Lewis's own:

> When your patient goes to church . . . he sees the local grocer with rather an oily expression on his face. . . . When he gets to his pew and looks round him he sees just that selection of his neighbors which he has hitherto avoided. . . . At his present stage, you see, he has an idea of Christians which is largely pictorial. Never let him ask what he expected them to look like. Keep everything hazy in his mind now, and you will have all eternity wherein to amuse yourself by producing the particular kind of clarity which Hell affords.[4]

Lewis says that in writing *Screwtape* he needed no guide to temptation other than his own heart. Clearly he had some difficulty converting his love of God into love of neighbor. But we learn in *Mere Christianity* of how Lewis arrived at a way of handling the problem:

> The rule for all of us is perfectly simple. Do not waste time bothering about whether you "love" your neighbor; act as if you did. When you are behaving as if you loved someone, you will presently come to love him. . . .[5]

Here and elsewhere Lewis makes it plain that living the Christian life is less a matter of thinking than of doing: a matter of pushing against our natural human dispositions, chipping away at faults, disciplining the self with toughness and perseverance and often without consolation. A further difficulty about doing it is that it is done in secret; there is often no one to praise us for it except the Lord. Then we notice how much our wish to do good was in order to earn the acclaim of others: to be thought good rather than to be good. This realization (which we make only now and then) humbles us. In the words of T. S. Eliot, we "do the right thing for the wrong reason." Our longing to be admired does not remove the goodness of the deeds done. But when we discover how unconverted our motivations still are, that is chastening. We—who were so bad before—learn to our sorrow that we are in danger of becoming like the Pharisee, dressing up in holy costumes and looking for front seats in the Temple!

Perhaps now I am projecting some of my own experience in the continuing conversion. But I think one thing we must learn after becoming serious as Christians is to fail for the Lord's sake. Humanly we desire success. It is tempting to blame this longing on modern values, but I suspect this problem has plagued human beings from the beginning. As Christians we must learn that success consists in choosing the Lord's way instead of our own. We must do again and again what we did in the very act of conversion; we must let go, unmake ourselves. We must learn that this unmaking is not a once-for-all choice but a learning that takes place only through practice and repetition.

The enthusiasm, the zeal of conversion, makes us want to be visible Christians: in the words of the hymn, to proclaim to the world what God has done. But a deeper understanding shows us that our Christianity must be invisible. Put another way, our turning must be so deep and real that we do it without seeking anything for ourselves. If our Christianity is to be visible—a light to the world—it must be because the Lord makes it visible, not because we ourselves seek to place it before the eyes of the world.

I would give Lewis's life as an example of this kind of invisible, inward conversion. I am not speaking now of Lewis the brilliant apologist, Lewis the debater, Lewis the writer of Christian mythologies for children. Certainly these were a part of Lewis's Christian commitment, a kind of witnessing. But I think the far more inspiring thing about Lewis's life is the way he lived.

He took on, for example, the responsibility for the mother and sister of a comrade who had died on the battlefield in World War I. He and the friend had swapped promises—to care for the other's relatives in case one was killed. Lewis survived and made good on his promise. The relationship was not an easy one. It placed many burdens upon Lewis that perhaps the care of his own parent might not have done. But he did it. I do not say he did it without ever grumbling or blowing off steam; but it was an enormous commitment of his time, his energy, and his life; this was a kind of lived charity that carried with it no promise of celebration or fame.

A second way in which Lewis lived out a commitment to practical charity was in his enormous correspondence with strangers. Through his writings, Lewis became a Christian model to many— an authority figure; people turned to him for pastoral counseling and advice. He was a busy man; he had no "obligation" to respond to this in the usual sense of that word. He must have perceived this barrage of correspondence as an imposition on his time, but also he perceived it as a call; and he answered it. Recently I heard an English clergyman say that he had known many notable Christian thinkers and lecturers in England who were contemporaries of Lewis. He thought that many of them talked a good game of Christianity, but did not live the Gospel in their personal lives. Lewis, he thought, by contrast, was credible: he did more than talk about Christianity; he lived it.

Fame, Milton says, is "the last infirmity of noble mind." Perhaps it is a bit old-fashioned to think of the desire for fame as a spiritual temptation. Certainly there is nothing wrong and everything right about using our natural talents as fruitfully as we can, and it is equally right and natural to expect to be recognized for them. But I think that there are definite spiritual pitfalls in wanting to do something big and noteworthy "for the Lord"; a risk that we might overlook something small and unimpressive (in the world's eyes), which might serve him just as well. Merton's worldly ambition was to be a great literary critic; after conversion, he aspired to be a great Christian literary critic; but Lax reminded him, rightly, that he ought to want to be a saint. Saints, on the whole, are people who did not do good in order to be famous, but became famous because of being good.

Is it unrealistic to want to be like this? All around us in the modern world there are examples of people who have done this very thing.

Teilhard de Chardin is a case in point. In today's perspective he seems a very fruitful Christian; his insights and vision have done much to heal the deep divisions between science and Christianity which have persisted since Galileo. He is also one of the few thinkers who has translated ancient Christian visions into terms that make sense in a divided world rushing towards apparent nuclear holocaust. And he seems now to have been considerably ahead of the rest of us in perceiving mysticism not as a byway but as a thoroughfare for modern believers. But Teilhard did not live to see his earthly work "completed." He died in what must have seemed to him (apart from his faith) obscurity and failure. And he did so partly because he had made an act of obedience and trust. When his vows of religious obedience asked of him that he bury his life's work, he did so willingly. He was willing to fail for the Lord if failure was what the Lord asked of him. This act of trust and faithfulness was—to use Bonhoeffer's phrase—costly discipleship. Teilhard did not only understand the meaning of the cross intellectually; he accepted it in his own life.

Bonhoeffer himself would be another example. Faithful to his own concept of discipleship, refusing to allow the grace of God to be sold "as cheapjack's wares," he witnessed through his own suffering to the truth of Christ, rather than yield to the coercions of the Hitler regime. His martyrdom may look glamorous in retrospect. But it could not have been so to him when he felt the noose around his neck.

In Hopkins we have another example. Here was a man who now seems to us a great Christian poet, but whose way in life excluded the literary success which might have been his in a different career. Hopkins was never comfortable or at ease in the work which his vocation as a Jesuit gave to him. As a teacher of church history and Latin he was poorly cast; but the role which was defined for the Jesuits of his time ruled out artistic work. But Hopkins persevered in the vision which the Lord had given him. At the time of his death he said, "I am so happy."

Mother Teresa of Calcutta, one of the world's most devoted Christians, has been featured on the cover of *Time* magazine. More recently she has been given a less ephemeral honor, the Nobel Peace Prize. I do not say she finds this recognition meaningless; but if her life ambition was to achieve either of these goals, she has certainly taken the long way around. In fact she chose an invisible career, giving her life away to bring life to others.

The work of Dorothy Day illustrates this, too. As we look back on her life, we see her as the founder and inspiration of the Catholic Worker movement. But in doing what she did she had no such perspective. Her commitment was made in plain trust, and work she chose had no promise of anything but obscurity. For all her natural drives to do something, the way she chose was not self-assertion but self-surrender.

All these Christians lived generous lives without the hope of being known for it. The fame came after the fact, was not the goal in the first place, nor was it the reward. And closer to home we can see examples of this same inward turning.

I recently came upon an example of this kind of commitment in a woman whose life I came to know about only after she died, through the memories of those who loved her. An adult convert, she devoted most of her life to Christian concerns. She poured herself out in practical charity, counseling and advising other people and just plain cheering them up; she made other people feel good about themselves. She devoted herself with great energy to her ailing mother, perhaps at the cost of greater personal enjoyment, or self-development, and she did so cheerfully. She died young—at least according to modern standards—and with a sense that she might have done more with her talents than she did; but she died loving the Lord and with a trusting acceptance of her own destiny. I never met her, yet I felt, in reading about her, as one does in reading the lives of the saints, that I wanted to be just like her.

The truth is that the Lord does ask each of us to do something radical and revolutionary: to give our lives to him as best we know how. But even after becoming Christians, we often want to define the terms on which our gift is to be made! The difficulty lies, sometimes, in responding to our own calls, the ones the Lord is really asking of us, especially the ones for which we are not so likely to be noticed and admired.

I speak now from my own experience. After I became a Christian I wished for a less worldly career; I wondered why God had not called me to some visibly Christian occupation; as I began to act out my Christianity, it seemed to me that I could do a better job of it if God had "sent" me—to serve the church or my fellowmen in some conspicuous way. Far from choosing his will, I was using my own daydreams about holiness as a way of resisting his will. I thought my wish was to be good for his sake. In fact I was resisting the less conspicuous call to be good in the work I already had. Following the opinion of the world, I doubted whether I could be holy unless I was engaged in some work which the world calls holy. It was some time before I came upon that quotation from Newman, "I shall be a preacher of truth in my own place"; still longer before I could accept or understand it. And the statement of Dorothy Sayers hit me very hard: "The only Christian work is good work well done."

As Christians we are called not only to be converted but also to convert the world. It was difficult for me sometimes to see that I could convert the world by remaining with it rather than by departing from it. I needed to learn, as Merton did after conversion, that the world we wish to be freed from is not "out there" but "in here."

Edward Rice, in his book *The Man in the Sycamore Tree*, describes this turning which Merton made after entering the monastery from hatred of the world to love of the world. In *The Seven Storey Mountain*, Merton had described how much the city of Louisville, Kentucky, had seemed to him symbolic of the ugliness and emptiness and false values of the world which he was leaving behind. Four years after its publication, Rice says, Merton was required to accompany the Vicar General of the Trappists, who spoke French but no English, into Louisville as an interpreter. Rice quotes from Merton's journal describing this experience: "I met the world and found it no longer so wicked after all. Perhaps the things I resented about the world when I left it were defects of my own that I had projected upon it. Now, on the contrary, everything stirred me with a deep and mute sense of compassion. . . . I went through the city, realizing for the first time in my life how good are all the people in the world and how much value they have in the sight of God."

After his first conversion—marked by his entrance into the Abbey at Gethsemani, Kentucky—Merton experienced many upheavals and subsequent turnings. His time of preparation for the priesthood was full of joy and consolation; the last chapters of *The Seven Storey Mountain* reflect the enthusiasm with which he accepted the monastic life, an acceptance which might make it seem that Merton's life after conversion would be one of equanimity and calm. Nothing could be further from the truth. Soon after ordination he was faced with a dryness not only in his spiritual life but in his creative and emotional life. Rice says: "He talks of 'abysmal testing and disintegration of my spirit,' which in December 1950, was replaced by 'completely new moral resources, a spring of new life, a peace and a happiness that I had never known before and which persisted in the face of nameless, interior terror.' Eventually," Rice says, "the peace grew, and the terror subsided and became an illusion." Throughout his life after conversion, Merton was subject to great emotional upheavals and spiritual trials, followed by floods of new insight and strengthening which caused him to say he was not the man he was before. Rice quotes him as follows: "Say that Merton is dead and never existed, and is a fake. Bogus Trappist exposed. . . ." And after his crisis in 1951 Merton wrote, "I have become very different from what I used to be. The man who began this journal (*The Sign of Jonas*) is dead, just as the man who finished *The Seven Storey Mountain* when this journal began is also dead, and what is more, the man who was the central figure in *The Seven*

Storey Mountain was dead over and over. . . . *The Seven Storey Mountain* is the work of a man I never even heard of."[6]

What seems to have happened after Merton's conversion is that the more he advanced in prayer, the more he identified with the world, not the world of world-flesh-devil but the world of human desperation and needs. Separated from the world's activism, he began to feel a call to witness in behalf of the poor and the victims of discrimination and injustice. He was also concerned that Christians in general were being encouraged to suppress these same impulses within themselves, to offer up their longings for a just order of things. He took the view that one must submit to an unjust world order only after trying to change it, rather than by a hopeless assumption that it cannot be changed. These movements of his spirit constantly placed Merton in a tension between his conscience and the monastic commitment he had made. But he spoke out through his writing. For a man who had voluntarily embraced silence, he had a good deal to say.

So Merton's experience in the continuing conversion suggests that the growth experience of conversion may be a stressful one. From a psychological viewpoint, Merton was a man under tension. Though God was central to his life, he was not free of despair and doubt.

In his late forties, Merton began to worry about death. (Non-Christians suppose that Christian faith removes this worry entirely!) He wrote in his journal, "I think I may die soon, though I am not exactly old." He was experiencing impatience and resentment. Much of his life in the monastery was difficult and frustrating. He applied for a transfer to another religious order and his request was refused. He sought to live a life of greater solitude; the way he went about it brought him into serious conflict with his superiors. At the same time, Rice says, Merton thought of himself as a "joyful" person! But Merton also complained at this time of his life that "an unexpected chill comes out of the depths; and I breathe the cold air of indifference, the sense of void."[7]

Do these statements by Merton suggest that he was ready to abandon either his religious vocation or his Christianity? Possibly they might; there are some who believe that when he left Gethsemani to travel to the Far East he was intending to leave for the last time. But such times of darkness may also be part of the continuing experience of conversion. The condition of the Christian after conversion—or "in" conversion—is not a state of blissful equanimity. It is a state of tension between the human self and the ideal Christian yet to be. A Christian is a person always in the process of becoming, of turning, and there are places in his journey which may be filled with dryness and despair.

A non-believing friend of mine said to me recently that he envied my certainty. I almost laughed! There are days for every committed Christian when the pole of unbelief exerts its attraction once again, times when the suffering of friends or our own disappointments make us doubt the goodness of God. The choice once made must be made again. Romano Guardini says it better when he calls faith "controlled doubt." And J. B. Phillips says faith is a faculty which must be exercised in order to be kept in form.

In his sermon on "Christian Repentance," Newman has described the continuing conversion in these words:

> Let it not be supposed . . . that I think that in the lifetime of each one of us there is some clearly marked date at which he began to seek God, and from which he has served him faithfully. Repentance is a work carried on at diverse times, and but gradually and with many reverses perfected. Or rather—and without any change in the meaning of repentance, it is a work never complete, never entire, unfinished . . . we are *ever* but beginning; the most perfect Christian is to himself but a beginner, a penitent prodigal, who has squandered God's gifts, and comes to him to be tried over again, not as a son, but as a hired servant.[8]

This insight—that conversion is a lifetime of continuous turning— need not discourage us, however. It is consistent with what the most hopeful of modern psychologists have to tell us about the experience of adulthood for us all. Abraham Maslow has made a careful study of what he calls the self-actualizing person, the person who might once have simply been called "happy." He finds in such persons not a state of rest but a fundamental striving, not an equilibrium but a constant tension in pursuit of a distant goal.

A most appropriate image for this continual striving which is never resolved, yet never without hope, was suggested to me by an insightful fellow Christian, Burton Everist. His image for conversion was a spiral staircase. As we go up the stair our vision may be obscured repeatedly by each turning that we make; still another act of faith is needed until we have come around the circle; but then we are at another level, looking at things from a new vantage point; and the top of the staircase is always out of sight. We know only by faith that it is there.

It is this vision which animates the whole process of conversion, for in the Christian life we come to understand, almost to see, that our goal is not only in this life but beyond it, and that death, which others think of as the end of life, is to be part of our life experience: a passageway to a still longer corridor beyond.

But I don't want to put so much emphasis on the tension and striving of the Christian life that I make it seem like an anxious reaching for the impossible. It isn't. One of the first things we learn in our encounter with the Lord is to stop trying to impress him. In prayer and in fellowship we begin to experience his love for us concretely; and the more we get to know him the more we find that he is prepared to love us as we are. This experience of coming to know the Lord strikes me rather like the encounter between therapist and patient, which Carl Rogers describes in his book *On Becoming a Person*. When we first come to the Lord we try to hide behind our pretenses, to be some other person that we think we are supposed to be. But the more we get to know him, the more we discover that he has created us to be ourselves. And we discover this not all at once, but little by little. Like patients at the first therapy session, we blurt out to the Lord everything we have done that is hateful to ourselves, everything we hate ourselves for, fully expecting to be able to shock him. The Lord retains his composure. His compassion is inexhaustible. This was something we knew about him in advance, and we almost resented it (perhaps for a sibling's reason: "He acts that way with everybody, and I wanted to be his favorite one!"). But when we begin to experience that forgiveness personally, it no longer seems to matter that he offers it to the whole world; for each of us knows that the Lord is giving it "just" to him. In this encounter we become aware of the wonder of individuality. God has made me, I am unique, even with all my faults I am worthwhile; this kind of self-discovery is strengthening and restoring; loving the Lord makes it possible to love ourselves in ways that are constructive and healthy. We grow to know ourselves better in the light he pours into our lives; we come to see what it is that he loves in us, how pleasing we are to him.

In this encounter we come to see how right Newman is (and McCall does it too) to speak of conversion in terms of the returning prodigal. But in reflecting on that story, we ought to put the emphasis not so much on the repentance of the son as on the rejoicing of the father. The son came home ashamed, wanting to make reparation. The father thought instead of staging a celebration of his son's return.

So, on a very human level, conversion is a growth experience, rather like a healing process. In fact some people (I think of Ruth Carter Stapleton and John Powell in particular) have devoted their ministries to preaching the Lord as a healer of emotional wounds. This is certainly Scriptural. Christ, we are told, has come to heal the brokenhearted; he has come that we may have life and have it to the full. At the same time, Christianity is not some emotional wonder drug, as the trials and difficulties of many converted Christians show. Some of the great saints were never able, despite their closeness to the Lord, to overcome fully their own neurotic emotional dispositions. One of the greatest pitfalls for converts, I think, can come out of a mistaken feeling that, to witness adequately to God's power in their lives, they must give an outward appearance of strength and peacefulness at all times; they fear that to admit weakness will somehow discredit the faith they profess; this way of thinking results in an emotional cramping, a self-imposition of obligations never laid on us by the Lord. Those dearest to Jesus—in fact Jesus Christ himself—had moments of sadness, discouragement, even of despair. To pretend otherwise is to flee from reality rather than to face it as Christianity calls us to do.

It may seem odd, but I think one of the most striking characteristics of the continuing conversion is a growth in the ability to find pleasure in ordinary experience. As we come to know the Lord better, we see how much he has given us in life that is enjoyable. This seems odd only because of a false stereotype: Christians are "supposed" to be serious, straight-and-narrow folk, cautious about living just for one's own pleasure and enjoyment. But as we grow in the Christian life, we find that pleasure is given to us without our asking, from unexpected sources, in ways we could never have brought about if we had tried.

Growth in the Christian life can give us a heightened perception of the good that is in others; the good that is all around us. When we are striving humanly for success and achievement (Christians must do this as much as anyone else), we can miss the pleasures of ordinary experience. In Thornton Wilder's *Our Town*, Emily asks the Stage Manager why people don't enjoy life while they're actually living it, and a thousand Hallmark greeting cards have advised us that we ought to do just that. But anxiety and self-centeredness prevents us. We can't find pleasure in life by trying to! But by giving ourselves away, surrender by surrender, in the experience of conversion, by resting in the Lord rather than in ourselves, a new consciousness of his creation—rather like what we had as children—sometimes comes back to us.

These pleasures are not within our command, however. They come in stabs and sudden bursts, not continually. God gives them to us and sometimes he withholds them from us. As we come nearer to the Lord we come nearer to understanding that both the moments of heightened pleasure and the takings away are gifts from him, part of the way that he is leading and drawing us to himself. To the extent that we try to capture and repeat our pleasures, they dry up and their consolations evaporate. But when we give ourselves to him, he gives us back something we could never effect in our own lives. Wordsworth speaks of joy in nature as Intimations of Immortality. Lewis built a whole personal theology around this experience which he called Joy. The moments of heightened perceptions which come to us—in prayer, in love, in friendship, in sorrow, in grief—all these moments seem to be signs of a life beyond our life, a life which the Lord is calling us to.

I do not mean to suggest that these blessings come to all Christians equally or in all times of their lives. An honest look at experience will convince us otherwise. But they do come at intervals in lives which are disposed towards God. And this disposition—this kind of affirmative response and openness in our lives—seems to be more than a matter of following our natural bent. It is an openness that comes instead by a consistent application of the self to the Christian life: by discipleship.

Perhaps the greatest gift given to me after conversion was the advice I had from Father Anthony Woods, the priest who instructed me for my reception into the Roman Catholic Church. It was he who convinced me that I couldn't take my conversion for granted; the continual application of myself to the Christian life would be my responsibility. He advised me to receive the sacraments often; to be confirmed promptly; to remember that the gift I had been given was worth guarding and caring for.

With the zeal of the convert I gladly took up most of the obligations of discipleship. But I think the one that slipped away from me, somehow, was prayer. For a long time I envied those whose life-style was devoted to prayer; for whom prayer was the basic business of living. I envied them, I longed to be like them, I told myself I would be like them if I could. In this way I allowed Screwtape and Wormwood to back me into rather a bad corner. I thought how nice it would be to pray if only I were anybody else but me. But being myself, naturally, it was impossible.

So, through something which looked to me like humility and an honest appraisal of my own limitations, I did something fairly prideful. I stopped praying, or perhaps didn't ever quite start. It was only a small omission, I thought to myself. I still went to church; received the sacraments with a certain regularity; read the Scriptures from time to time and did a good bit of reading *about* Scripture (not always, by the way, the same thing as reading Scripture itself, just as reading about praying is not the same as praying); took all the appropriate Catholic journals and worked out my own viewpoints on moral issues facing Christians (if any high-level commission had needed my opinion, I was ready); and I prayed mostly in distress, when faced with personal crises, in desperation.

What I did not do was develop a day-to-day dialogue with the Lord, a habit of prayer which would become part of the rhythm of each day.

I found, after a while, to my dismay, that I had become very adept at talking to everybody else *but* the Lord, talking to other people *about* the Lord. It was rather like those conversations one sometimes has, in which a friend reports that she has seen a friend who said how much she missed you, and was intending to call you up for lunch one of these days; when all the friend actually has to do is pick up the phone.

I don't know why I got out of the habit of prayer, or never really formed it, for I knew, from my first experience as a Christian, that it could be done. I think, in some ways, it was a lack of confidence, a fear, perhaps, that nothing in particular would be changed, that nothing would really "happen" if I did. But at some point I began to feel this as a definite lack in my life, a need, even a call. I began to remember some of my early talks with Father Moore about prayer. Especially I could hear him saying, so firmly: "A Lent missed is a year lost from the spiritual life."

I think I heard his voice saying that for more than one Lent before I answered that particular call. But there did come a Lent which was the time for still a further turning: I began to take up the habit of prayer. I do not pretend it is always rewarding, or easy. But I have come to feel that without it, I would be walking straight into a stone wall.

There are more steps beyond me on the spiral staircase which I have yet to climb; and I am, as Newman put it, *ever* but beginning. But, if there is one word I have to offer to those who have made the first turning, it is to watch carefully at every bend along the way.

It is helpful, too, to have others to watch with you. Very few of us are strong enough or sane enough to advance in the Christian life without the support and help of others. Directors, prayer groups, fellow Christians, the faith of others and their insights strengthen us, keep us out of trouble, illuminate the way. The road is tough going sometimes; I think we need the help of other believers or we may stumble and fall.

There is another value in these kinds of relationships, I think. It is hard for us to measure our own progress in the spiritual life. We feel, often, that we are not getting anywhere. But when we watch others around us grow in holiness—and unable to see themselves growing—it helps us to believe that we are growing too.

Some thirty years after the publication of *The Seven Storey Mountain*, Merton wrote:

> We are not converted only once in our lives, but many times; and this endless series of large and small conversions, inner revolutions, leads to our transformation in Christ. But while we may have the generosity to undergo one or two such upheavals, we cannot face the necessity of further and greater rendings of our inner self, without which we cannot finally become free.[9]

To yield again and again to the calls God gives us, to come up higher when we are humanly convinced we have gone as high as we can go, this takes a special kind of courage. It seems quite beyond us! But even as I say this, I hear Bob Lax saying to Merton on a summer's night on Sixth Avenue, "Don't you believe that God can make you a saint if you consent to let him do it?" After each miracle God works in our lives, we may be grateful, but we are inclined to shut the door after it, as though one or two miracles were all one could expect, or tolerate, in one lifetime. But the Lord, more often than not, has something else in mind for us. As soon as we have caught our breath, he is asking us to start climbing again.

So we experience a third and a fourth conversion more amazing than the first; and after each one we resolve that the next time we won't be so surprised. In time, for some of us, there comes a kind of tolerance of miracle that we did not have before: a growing acceptance of the love that will not let us go. Slowly, we begin to rest in the knowledge that rescue is not an occasional event in our experience of God but the whole and fundamental way he is dealing with us. He means to have us; he means to bring us to himself; the Lord who left the ninety-nine to find us in the first place is willing to chase us down again and again; and does so. No suffering is too deep for him to turn it into a blessing, a grace that frees us and draws us closer to him.

We come, then, as this life of God grows in us, to acquire a kind of dual vision: an eye that sees the outward reality of things and the inward reality all at once; a kind of transparency develops in our perception of others and the world itself. It is as though every event were lit up from within, and the life of God made visible even in our sufferings; we come to accept and even to desire the darknesses of our experience as tokens of our onward movement in the way.

I cannot help comparing the Lewis who was "dragged through a doorway"—pulled through the high gates kicking and screaming—with the Lewis who preached "The Weight of Glory" more than a decade later. The man who found immortality something of an unfair inducement now talks about it with a shameless and unabashed delight; to be sure, he says he feels a certain shyness about doing so, but that seems to be one of the literary conceits, one of the tactics he is using to open the hearts of his listeners; he even admits that he is doing just that; the man who once said he was never less sure of a doctrine than when he had just successfully defended it is now deliberately weaving a spell, using every resource of imagery he has to quicken others' longings for the vision of God. It seems to me that in a few short years he has moved so far, has grown so much, has experienced God so definitely in his own life, that he has no qualms about awakening our dreams of bliss. "All the leaves of the New Testament are rustling with the rumor . . ." he tells us, that heaven is real and that we shall get in. And in the same breath the man who (for I assume this was Lewis himself) could not face the oily grocer in the next pew is telling us of his growing love for ordinary men and women. They are on their way to being gods and goddesses, he says, at least some of them are. "Next to the Blessed Sacrament itself, your neighbor is the holiest object presented to your senses." For Christ, Lewis says, is hidden in him.

Lewis is not the only Christian in whom we can see this striking transformation: conversion. Divinization, as Teilhard calls it, is happening wherever men and women are open to it. When we consent, the power of God breaks through.

I have spoken of the experience of conversion entirely in Christian terms: of necessity, because I have written of my own experience and the way that I—in company with a few spiritual mentors and friends—have traveled. But I think it is important to say that I do not regard conversion as a specifically Christian experience.

Conversion—being a matter of discovering the reality of God—occurs in all times and places, in all religions and outside of religion as well.

I cannot speak with authority of this meeting within Judaism, within Buddhism or Islam. But I am confident that it is taking place. To say anything else would be to place limitations on the power of God, to set constraints on his love.

I am aware, too, of marvelous goodness in people who do not profess any religion, for whom religion is without meaning, or who may be opposed to religion and regard it as a destructive and negative force in human affairs. However much I differ with their judgments, however much I regret not being able to share my faith with them, I must feel that the Holy Spirit is at work in every good heart. I spoke recently with an unbelieving friend of mine of the goodness I can feel working in human friendship, and called it the work of the Holy Spirit. She felt it too, but said, "Why do you have to call it that? Why can't you just say it's natural goodness, goodness that's just part of human beings?" For her, to call this force for good by any religious name was to spoil it, to make it less real. Atheists wonder why we Christians always have to drag in God to explain things, a *deus ex machina* to make the plot work when human invention fails. I respect this annoyance and sense that some of it, at least, may be due to the real transgressions of Christians who have beat others about the head with their religious opinions and have used God's rules as a way of making others feel inadequate. Perhaps, by our attitudes, we have made God seem less desirable to others than he does to us. Perhaps it is heartless of us to try to change such viewpoints. Could it be that atheists need to disbelieve in God as much as we need to believe in him?

With regard to other religions, it is worth mentioning that two of the converted Christians of this book, Bede Griffiths and Thomas Merton, came, as the years passed, to a Christianity which draws on Eastern enlightenment: a world-embracing Christianity. Griffiths has recently written a book, *Return to the Center*, the fruit of many years as a Christian contemplative in India, which relates the Christian vision to other spiritualities and finds a common thread in them. Merton was drawn to Eastern spirituality as well. At the time of his death he was visiting the Far East, and it is thought that he may have wanted to remain there. Perhaps the most significant—at least to me—of modern Christians in this regard is Teilhard, whose vision, approached through the sciences as well as his personal spirituality, was of a world and a creation reaching towards integration and oneness, a world shot through with the presence of Christ and becoming unified in him.

In this perspective, the modern movements towards spiritual unity seem less like the work of human beings struggling for doctrinal agreement and more like the work of the Spirit within us, healing and enlightening, integrating the whole of creation. In human terms, such dreams as Christian unity and world peace seem totally naive. It is only through trust that God himself is at work in the world that we hope for the things that history suggests we should not hope for.

For myself, the Afterwards has been an experience of growing reconciliation. Like Merton looking back on Louisville, Kentucky, I have looked back on the religion left behind, Christian Science, and have come to see both Christ and science in it. Fifteen years ago I could not understand how Mrs. Eddy could have presumed to set the Eucharist aside. Today I think I understand that. In fact, I am sure that the Lord first spoke to me in Christian Science, in ways that were simple, clear, and unforgettable. In the church I grew up in, there were three inscriptions and only three: the words of Jesus promising that our prayers would be answered; the words of John the Evangelist, "God is love"; and the words of Mrs. Eddy, "Divine love always has met and always will meet every human need." Everywhere in her hymns I see the person of Jesus Christ, healing the sick, calming the tempest, comforting the comfortless. And I identify deeply with the clear conviction of Christian Scientists that nothing is impossible with God.

In the Mormon Church I see a powerful witness to God's continuing willingness to share his life with men. In the Jehovah's Witnesses I quicken to the conviction that God is acting in history and time. In Judaism I respond to the faithfulness of God and the beauty of the Law. And in atheism and agnosticism I respond to each person's need to live the truth as he or she sees it, faithful to personal insights and to conscience.

Beyond that is a mystery. Why should the God who is so real and personal to some be so unreal and implausible to others, when all other things—reason, intellect, openness to experience—appear to be equal? I can't say.

I only know it is my faith that God is at work in our lives even when we can't see it. This happens of course for believers as well.

For some of the things we can't account for in reality, we have had to invent terminology. This unaccountable action which seems to occur in the most arbitrary way—this infusion of the knowledge of God into the personal lives of some of us—comes by what Christians call "grace." Theologians are even able to sort it out into several different types, which is not quite the same as understanding it.

For myself, I prefer Bede Griffiths' metaphor: the golden string. For myself, I am glad that it was put in my hand and I had the strength to follow it.

I don't believe or expect that my way must be another's way. I am told that in the Orient men of faith, when meeting one another, ask, "What worthy path do you follow?" That question seems to imply the validity of every path good men and women take towards wisdom and enlightenment.

It is my faith that the love of Jesus Christ is stirring in all of them; and I can't be easily shaken from that conviction. I know, too, that it is possible to be offered the love of Christ, to know it for what it is, and to refuse it; but I'm not inclined to think that very many people have done so.

Perhaps the question isn't worth another moment's speculation. Something, after all, must be left up to God and his own unfathomable ways of dealing with us all.

NOTES

1 : TURNING

1. Lines attributed to William Blake, Bede Griffiths, *The Golden String* (New York: P. J. Kenedy & Sons, 1954), p. 9.
2. Thomas Merton, *The Seven Storey Mountain* (Garden City, N.Y.: Image Books, 1970), pp. 262–63.
3. Galatians 2:20, The New American Bible.
4. Evelyn Underhill, *Practical Mysticism* (New York: E. P. Dutton, 1915), pp. 33–34.
5. John McCall, "Psychological Dimensions of Conversion," NCR Cassette.
6. Merton, op. cit., pp. 289–90.
7. Carl R. Rogers, *On Becoming a Person* (Boston: Houghton Mifflin, 1961), p. 26.
8. C. S. Lewis, *Mere Christianity* (New York: Macmillan, 1943), p. 86.

2 : DESIRE

1. Gordon Allport, *The Individual and His Religion* (New York: Macmillan, 1950), p. 20.

2. Griffiths, op. cit., p. 10.

3. Merton, op. cit., p. 19.

4. C. S. Lewis, *Surprised by Joy: The Shape of My Early Life* (New York: Harcourt Brace Jovanovich, 1955), p. 7.

5. ———, *The Pilgrim's Regress: An Allegorical Apology for Christianity, Reason and Romanticism* (Grand Rapids, Michigan: William B. Eerdmans, 1958), p. 7.

6. ———, *Surprised by Joy*, p. 18.

7. Griffiths, op. cit., p. 10.

8. Ibid., p. 11.

9. Ibid., p. 10.

10. William Wordsworth, *Ode: Intimations of Immortality from Recollections of Early Childhood*, in Edward Perkins, ed. *English Romantic Writers* (New York: Harcourt Brace Jovanovich, 1967).

11. Merton, op. cit., p. 142.

12. William Wordsworth, *Tintern Abbey*.

13. Lewis, *The Pilgrim's Regress*, p. 10.

14. *The Confessions of St. Augustine*, trans., John K. Ryan (Garden City, N.Y.: Image Books), p. 43.

3 : DIALECTIC

1. Avery Dulles, *A Testimonial to Grace* (New York: Sheed & Ward, 1946), p. 13.

2. Ibid., p. 21.

3. Ibid., p. 22.

4. Ibid., p. 24.

5. Ibid., p. 25.

6. Ibid., p. 26.

7. Ibid., pp. 26–27.

8. Ibid., p. 29.

9. Ibid., p. 39

10. Griffiths, op. cit., p. 51.

11. Lewis, *Surprised by Joy*, p. 171.

12. Ibid., p. 174.

13. Ibid., pp. 180–81.

14. Dulles, op. cit., pp. 50–51.

15. Ibid., p. 52.

16. Ibid., p. 54.

17. Ibid., p. 54.

18. Mary Baker Eddy, *Science and Health with Key to the Scriptures*, The Christian Science Publishing Society, 1906.

19. Ibid., p. 313.

20. Robert Graves, *The White Goddess: a Historical Grammar of Poetic Myth* (New York: Octagon Books, a division of Farrar, Straus and Giroux, 1976), p. 242.

4 : STRUGGLE

1. Lewis, *Surprised by Joy*, p. 206.

2. Ibid., p. 214.

3. Ibid., p. 216.

4. Walter Hooper, ed., *They Stand Together: The Letters of C. S. Lewis to Arthur Greeves* (New York: Macmillan, 1979), p. 425.

5. Ibid., p. 427.

6. Lewis, *Surprised by Joy*, pp. 223–24.

7. Letter to A. K. Hamilton Jenkin, quoted in Roger Lancelyn Green and Walter Hooper, *C. S. Lewis: a Biography* (New York and London: Harcourt Brace Jovanovich, 1974), p. 106.

8. Lewis, *Surprised by Joy*, p. 225.

9. Merton, *The Seven Storey Mountain*, p. 218.

10. Ibid., p. 221.

11. Ibid., p. 225.

12. Ibid., p. 238.

13. Ibid., p. 249.

14. Ibid., p. 252.

15. Lewis, *The Four Loves* (New York: Harcourt Brace, 1960), p. 179.

16. Merton, *The Seven Storey Mountain*, p. 140.

17. Griffiths, *The Golden String*, p. 92.

18. Ibid., p. 93.

19. Ibid., pp. 93–97.

20. Dorothy Day, *The Long Loneliness* (Garden City, N.Y.: Image Books, 1959), p. 128.

21. Ibid., p. 130.

22. Ibid., p. 132.

23. Ibid., p. 134.

24. Gilbert L. Oddo, ed., *These Came Home: The Odyssey of Fifteen Converts* (Milwaukee, Wisconsin: Bruce Publishing Co., 1954), pp. 97–98.

5: SURRENDER

1. Griffiths, op. cit., p. 97.
2. Lewis, *Surprised by Joy*, p. 231.
3. G. K. Chesterton, *The Catholic Church and Conversion* (New York: Macmillan, 1961), p. 65.
4. Ibid., p. 63.
5. John McCall, "Psychological Dimensions of Conversion," NCR Cassette.
6. Lewis, *Surprised by Joy*, p. 228.
7. Romans 6:3, New American Bible.
8. Lewis, *Surprised by Joy*, p. 180.
9. Ibid., p. 229.
10. Ibid., p. 224.
11. William James, *The Varieties of Religious Experience* (New York: Macmillan, 1961), p. 177.
12. Ibid., pp. 177–78.
13. Merton, *The Seven Storey Mountain*, p. 310.
14. Edmond Rostand, *Cyrano de Bergerac*, (New York: Bantam, 1978), pp. 188–89.

6: AFTERWARDS

1. Charles Dickens, *A Christmas Carol* (London: Chapman and Hall, 1843), pp. 157–60.
2. Lewis, *Poems* (New York: Harcourt Brace Jovanovich, 1977), p. 128.
3. Dulles, op. cit., pp. 117–18.
4. Lewis, *The Screwtape Letters* (New York: Macmillan, 1961), pp. 12–13.
5. Lewis, *Mere Christianity* (New York: Macmillan, 1960), p. 116.
6. Edward Rice, *The Man in the Sycamore Tree* (New York: Doubleday, 1970), p. 76.
7. Ibid., p. 118.
8. John Henry Newman, "On Christian Repentance" in *Parochial and Plain Sermons*, Vol. III (London: Longmans, Green & Co., 1899), p. 90.
9. Thomas Merton, letter published in *Information Catholiques Internationale*, April 1973, back cover.

ADDITIONAL READINGS ON CONVERSION

Chapters 1 and 2: *Turning and Desire*

Allport, Gordon. *The Individual and His Religion.* Macmillan, 1970.
A psychologist reflects on the nature of the religious quest and the yearning for God.

Barth, Karl. "The Awakening to Conversion," chapter in *Church Dogmatics,* included in Conn, Walter E., ed., *Conversion: Perspectives on Personal and Social Transformation.* Alba House, 1978.
In this chapter, Barth suggests that in conversion the "old man" and "new man" exist side by side in a continuing tension.

Chesterton, G. K. *The Catholic Church and Conversion.* Macmillan, 1961.
An excellent discussion of conversion from a specifically Roman Catholic viewpoint. Conversion is described not only as a faith choice but as a specific movement towards Roman Catholicism.

Conn, Walter E., ed. *Conversion: Perspectives on Personal and Social Transformation.* Alba House, 1978.
Conn has gathered many perspectives from modern Protestant and Catholic sources on the nature of conversion and the changes it brings about.

Graham, Billy. *Christian Conversion* (pamphlet). Billy Graham Evangelistic Association, 1959.

A brief, concise, and thorough definition of Christian conversion.

Haughton, Rosemary. *The Transformation of Man.* Templegate, 1967.
Theological reflections on the lifelong difference made by Christianity.

James, William. *The Varieties of Religious Experience.* Macmillan, 1961.
The chapters devoted to "the divided self" and conversion relate to the initial turning; later chapters on saintliness and mysticism provide insights on the continuing experience of conversion.

Johnson, Paul E. *Psychology of Religion.* Abingdon Press, 1959.
See chapter on "Conversion."

Lepp, Ignace. *Health of Mind and Soul.* Doubleday, 1966.
A contemporary French priest and psychologist, himself a convert to Christianity, discusses religious belief in the light of clinical experience. ·

Lonergan, Bernard. *Method in Theology.* Herder and Herder, 1972.
See chapter entitled "Dimensions of Conversion." Lonergan is considered one of the most important contemporary thinkers on conversion.

Oates, Wayne. *The Psychology of Religion.* Word Books, 1973.
See chapter entitled "Conversion: Sacred and Secular." Oates examines a number of different examples of spiritual turning. His discussion of Alcoholics Anonymous as conversion experience is brief but excellent.

Pratt, James Bissett. *The Religious Consciousness.* Hafner Press, 1971.
Republication of an early work on conversion (Macmillan, 1924) which deals with the religious quest and the desire for God in a psychological perspective.

Sheen, Fulton. *Peace of Soul.* McGraw-Hill, 1949.
Archbishop Sheen, especially during the time of his television ministry, was credited with many conversions. While in this book he may go too far in estimating the psychological benefits of conversion, his chapters "The Psychology of Conversion" and "The Theology of Conversion" are among the best discussions on the subject.

Starbuck, E. D. *Psychology of Religion.* Charles Scribner's, 1899.
One of the earliest studies of adolescent religious conversion. Many of James's insights are based on it.

Chapter 3: *Dialectic*

Adler, Mortimer. "The Problem of Proving God's Existence." Unpublished, 1978.
    In this lecture, Dr. Adler advances the idea that both atheism and belief are faith positions.
——. *How to Think About God*. Macmillan, 1980.
    A discussion which is sharply restricted to arguments based on reason.
Casserley, J. V. Langmead. *No Faith of My Own*. Longmans, 1950.
    A concise statement of Christian belief by an Anglican.
Chesterton, G. K. *The Everlasting Man*. Image Books, 1955.
    Chesterton uses his formidable resources of faith, intellect, and imagination to make Christian faith intelligible to his contemporaries.
——. *Orthodoxy*. Image Books.
    Written when Chesterton was an Anglican, this faith statement is an articulate exposition and defense of traditional Christian thought.
Graves, Robert. *The White Goddess*. Octagon Books, 1976.
    Subtitled A *Historical Grammar of Poetic Myth*, this book is not an attack on religion or Christianity. But in articulating elements of mythology in Christian history, belief, and ritual, Graves raises some difficulties for thoughtful believers.
Guardini, Romano. *The Faith and Modern Man*. Henry Regnery, 1965.
    An exposition of a number of Catholic faith positions for the modern reader. Of particular interest is the chapter entitled "Faith and Doubt in the Stages of Life."
Hick, John, ed. *The Existence of God*. Macmillan, 1964.
    A truly comprehensive book of readings on arguments for the existence of God: ontological, cosmological, teleological, and moral, among others. Readings are from noted thinkers throughout the centuries, including Anselm, Aquinas, Kant, Kierkegaard. "Both" sides of the issues are examined.
Huxley, Julian. *Religion Without Revelation*. Mentor, 1957.
    This renowned biologist, and member of a famous scientific family of antireligious sympathies, explains some of his doubts about traditional religion and suggests hopeful humanist strategies for the future.
Lepp, Ignace. *Atheism in Our Time*. Macmillan, 1963.
    Lepp draws an experiential picture of atheism and atheists

based on clinical and personal experience as well as currents of thought.

Lewis, C. S. *Mere Christianity*. Macmillan, 1975.
This collection of broadcast talks given in Great Britain is enjoying a new popularity in the United States. It is a concise statement of Christian belief which cuts across denominational lines.

Montagu, Ashley. *Immortality, Religion and Morals*. Hawthorn Books, 1971.
Belief in immortality is seen as a defense mechanism against death and an obstacle to social progress.

Russell, Bertrand. *Why I Am Not a Christian*. Simon and Schuster, 1957.
A concise exposition of Russell's logic with regard to God's existence and other religious viewpoints.

Sayers, Dorothy L. *The Mind of the Maker*. Harper & Row, 1979.
Sayers uses the creative act of the artist as an analogue for the creative act of God the Father: a fascinating intellectual exploration of the nature of God as Mind.

Chapters 4 and 5:
Struggle and Surrender: Personal Conversion Stories

Augustine. *Confessions*. Penguin, 1961.
The model conversion story in many eyes, it is a movement both intellectual and intuitive in nature.

Bunyan, John. *Grace Abounding*. Oxford University Press, 1962.
A very moving account of Bunyan's own spiritual baptism: both his death to sin and his tearful rising into new life in God.

Cavanaugh, Arthur. *My Own Back Yard*. Guild Press, 1966.
A writer is converted as an adult to the religion of his youth.

Cogley, John. *A Canterbury Tale*. Seabury Press, 1976.
Subtitled *Experiences and Reflections 1916–1976*, this is the account of Cogley's experience as a Catholic writer and activist and especially his movement to Anglicanism late in life.

Colson, Charles. *Born Again*. Bantam, 1977.
Written with a sincerity that confounds many who disbelieved Colson's conversion.

Day, Dorothy. *The Long Loneliness*. Image Books, 1959.
A deeply moving personal account, one of the model conversion stories of this book.

Dulles, Avery. *A Testimonial to Grace*. Sheed & Ward, 1946.
Written some years after Dulles became a believer and a Roman

Catholic, and after his entrance into the Society of Jesus. Dulles's conversion is one of the models of this book.

Griffiths, Bede. *The Golden String.* P. J. Kenedy & Sons, 1954.
Written some years after Griffiths' conversion (1931) and his entrance into the monastic life (1932) and his ordination to the priesthood (1947), it nevertheless seems to reflect complete recall of his intellectual and spiritual progress and most particularly his reading. If it is nothing else, the book itself is a spiritual reading list. Also a model conversion for the present volume.

Hopkins, Gerard Manley. *A Selection from His Poems and Prose.* Penguin, 1963.
Hopkins did not write a spiritual autobiography, but some of his letters which are included in this volume show clearly some dimensions of the conversion crisis and surrender.

Knox, Ronald. *A Spiritual Aeneid.* Sheed & Ward, 1958.
A record of the movement Knox made first into the Anglican priesthood and later into the Roman Catholic priesthood, and the enormous intricacies of such a passage.

Lepp, Ignace. *From Karl Marx to Jesus Christ.* Sheed & Ward, 1958.
Lepp describes first his youthful conversion to Marxism and his later conversion to Christianity and Catholicism.

Lewis, C. S. *The Pilgrim's Regress.* Eerdmans, 1958.
While Lewis denied that this allegorical tale was an account of his own conversion, the resemblances are there.

———. *Surprised by Joy: the Shape of My Early Life,* Harcourt Brace, 1955.
Lewis's conversion is straightforwardly told, and the shape of conversion can also be seen from it. This conversion and Lewis's reflections on it are the models for my own thinking about conversion.

Marshall, Catherine. *A Man Called Peter.* Avon, 1971.
The story of how a young Scot responded to God's call; like all conversion stories, a love story, told beautifully by his widow.

Merton, Thomas. *The Seven Storey Mountain.* Image Books, 1970.
Merton's own account of his call to conversion and holiness; one of the model conversions of this volume.

Newman, John Henry. *Apologia Pro Vita Sua.* Image Books, 1956.
A classic account of a conversion, a turning experienced first as an Anglican and then as a Roman Catholic.

Oddo, Gilbert, ed. *These Came Home.* Bruce, 1954.
A collection of personal accounts of conversion by fifteen men and women, showing remarkable parallels.

Powell, John. *He Touched Me*. Argus, 1974.
  A personal account of conversion in childhood, again in adolescence, and finally in adult life.

Chapter 6: *Afterwards: the Continuing Conversion*

Bonhoeffer, Dietrich. *The Cost of Discipleship*. Macmillan, 1963.
  Bonhoeffer makes it plain that the Christian life must cost us something.
Griffiths, Bede. *Return to the Center*. Templegate, 1977.
  The fruit of many years in the contemplative life, the last twenty-odd years in India, this book is Griffiths' sharing of insights into several spiritual traditions; he sees Christ in them all.
Lewis, C. S. A *Grief Observed*. Bantam, 1976.
  Lewis's response to the death of his wife shows the ongoing struggle which occurs in a man's relationship with God.
Maslow, Abraham. *Toward a Psychology of Being*. D. Van Nostrand, 1968.
  Many of Maslow's insights, while not specific to conversion, enlighten us with regard to adult maturation, reaching for distant goals, and growth experience.
May, Rollo. *Love and Will*. Dell, 1969.
  Validates, from modern clinical experience, much that the spiritual writers of past times have told us about growth in spirituality and personal maturation.
Merton, Thomas. *The Sign of Jonas*. Image Books, 1956.
  Merton's spiritual journal suggests that the work of conversion-after-conversion is not easy but has moments of great joy and wonder.
Tournier, Paul. *The Adventure of Living*. Harper & Row, 1965.
  While it does not use conversion terminology, this discussion of life as a day-to-day spiritual journey is about the continuing conversion which Christians experience.
Underhill, Evelyn. *Practical Mysticism*. Dutton, 1915.
  This Anglican writer and mystic suggests that the direct encounter with God is within the reach of "ordinary" persons in ordinary life-styles.

INDEX

Agnosticism, 16, 17, 87

Allport, Gordon, 32

Anglican, Anglo-Catholic, Church of England, 41, 44, 53, 75, 76, 108, 119, 145, 146, 147, 153

Asceticism, 103, 116

Atheist, Atheism, 16, 17, 59, 70, 84, 87, 94, 100, 123, 173, 175

Augustine, 48, 51, 55, 63, 103, 130

Catholic (belief, churches, creeds), 21, 42, 44, 69, 81, 107, 108, 125, 145, 147, 155, 161

Chesterton, G. K., 16, 44, 91, 109, 130, 131, 138, 143

Christian Science, 43, 44, 71, 73, 74, 75, 174

Conscience, 77, 92, 164

Contrition, 37, 111, 113, 114

Baptism, 104, 125, 145, 146, 148

Barth, Karl, 156–57

Bible, 18, 66, 67, 73, 91, 121, 148

Bonhoeffer, Dietrich, 160

Book of Common Prayer, The, 40, 41, 117, 146

Day, Dorothy, Throughout; see *especially* chapter 4

Death, 35, 36, 43, 86, 90, 114

Discipleship, 160, 169

Dulles, Avery, Throughout; see *especially* chapter 3

Eddy, Mary Baker, 43, 182
Episcopal Church, 75; see Anglican, Anglo-Catholic, Church of England
Eucharist, 41, 44–45, 95, 96, 146, 148

Fasting, 116, 121
Frazer, Sir James, 67, 85, 86, 100

Grace, 21, 24, 36, 65, 95, 123, 130, 141, 147, 152, 172, 175
Graves, Robert, 67, 84, 85
Griffiths, Bede, Throughout; see especially chapters 2, 4, and 5

Holiness, 30, 45, 61, 62, 103, 104, 108, 115, 162, 171
Hopkins, Gerard Manley, 16, 20, 153, 160
Huxley, Julian, 43, 84, 85, 86

Immortality, 42, 59, 84, 86, 90, 137

James, William, 25, 27, 28, 139, 141, 142

King James Translation, Version, 18, 79
Knox, Ronald, 83

Lewis, C. S., Throughout

McCall, John, 23, 24, 132, 133, 167
Marshall, Peter, 25
Maslow, Abraham, 165
Merton, Thomas, Throughout
Metanoia, 29
Miracle, 66, 68, 73, 78, 152, 171
Monastic life, 17, 116, 122, 132, 144, 152, 164
Montagu, Ashley, 84, 85, 86
Mystical, Mysticism, 74, 102, 104, 129, 155, 160
Myth, Mythology, 49, 62, 66, 67, 84, 85, 98, 99, 159

Neurotic, Neurosis, 48, 92, 93, 122
Newman, John Henry, 16, 20, 132, 133, 147, 165, 167
Nostalgia, 32, 37, 38, 42, 44, 45, 46, 109

Peak experience, 37, 151
Prayer, 37, 104, 110, 114, 115, 116, 117, 118, 120, 121, 123, 124, 138, 152, 164, 169, 170
Priesthood, 143, 144

Real Presence, 146
Repentance, 112, 116, 117, 120, 165, 167
Revelation, 15, 72
Rogers, Carl, 25–26, 166
Roman Catholics, Roman Catholicism, Church of Rome, 17, 41, 67, 68, 69, 132, 145, 146, 147, 153, 169

Russell, Bertrand, 84, 85

Saint, Sanctity, 23, 121, 124, 141,
    147, 160, 162, 167, 171
Salvation, 108, 141, 154
Sayers, Dorothy L., 16, 162
Sheen, Fulton J., 28
Sin, Sinfulness, 36, 78, 110, 112,
    113, 116, 156

Teilhard de Chardin, Pierre, 44,
    160, 172, 174

Underhill, Evelyn, 22, 23

Will, 87, 113, 118
"Wreckage," 132, 153, 155